I0153556

# A Declaration of Inter-Dependence
## Seeing Eye to I

By
Brande Watson

Copyright © 2023 by Bransford Watson

All rights reserved. No part of this publication may be reproduced, distributed or transmitted in any form or by any means, electronic or mechanical, including photocopying, recording or by any information storage and retrieval system without permission in writing from the copyright owner.

Rights are administered by Pure Heart Publishing

Pure Heart Publishing
P. O. Box 2341
Atlanta, GA 30188
Web: www.PureHeartPublisher.com

This book was published in the United States of America
Pure Heart Publishing, Atlanta, GA. October, 2023

First Edition: October, 2023

Library of Congress Control Number: 2023918070
ISBN: 978-1-954008-05-2

# Table of Contents

# Prologue

Ponder for a minute how laboriously peoples in all civilizations in all corners of the world have recorded their lifestyles and world views in artful ways, such that it becomes the stuff of history. Then consider how painstakingly researchers in later generations have sought to uncover and interpret those records, to trace the mystic cords of collective memory.

Today because of these arts and sciences, you can trace these ties, which attest to your identity and uniqueness, in ways that are sometimes overt, sometimes subtle, family, ethnicity, religious traditions, national origins, appearance and social status. They teach you how you should feel, act, and relate to others. All too often, you may experience "dueling identities", creating internal conflict and confusion as to who you are.

Each of us came on the American scene amidst an ongoing drama when the stage was already set and action underway. At some point consciousness of our own individual existence began to stir within. We became aware that we had wants and needs, like others in some ways, special in other instances.

Perhaps the ultimate goal of a quality education is for each of us to know our true selves, to gain a deep sense of our similarities and differences. Our mission hereby is to consult the record of human experience as set forth by various resources; to apply logic and reason to our findings so that the data become intelligible; communicate with others to develop knowledge; learn diverse and shared values and objectives of the community to understand who we are, and to what we aspire. The spirit of our age, or zeitgeist, forms the backdrop from which we can discern a perspective of both our achievements and our challenges.

*Beneath the skin we are all kin,*
*The way to win is to look within.*

# Introduction

Throughout known history, man has demonstrated a propensity for being inhumane toward one another. By tallying up differences and assigning people to groups according to those man-made distinctions, one people group has developed intricate systems to make themselves feel superior and to relegate others to lowliness and subservience.

This programming has been applied across continents and throughout centuries and has become so commonplace as to be accepted fact. The "Illusionary truth effect" is the tendency to believe in false information after hearing it repeatedly. Or as Joseph Gorbbels said:
"If you tell a lie big enough and keep repeating it, people will eventually come to believe it."

That "Reiteration Effect" has certainly been applied in America. And we see it in all of our major institutions, including education, business, health, justice system, policing, agriculture, banking, military benefits, etc. if you're White, you're right, if you're Black, get back. This way of thinking is so ingrained in America, that many have come to consider it normal or inescapable.

The truth of the matter is, that there's only one race on the planet. That is the human race. Perhaps, we were given unique characteristics for us to battle it out, in our ignorance, and then come to the realization that we are one race of humans.

# Chapter 1: Mother Lucy
*E Unum Pluribus*

Hundreds of millions of years ago there was only one huge land mass on this planet. Then over millions of years a series of super massive volcanic explosion broke up that single massive unit into the continents that are known today. What we know as North and South America are still separating at a rate of several inches per year, widening the Atlantic Ocean. Europe separated from Africa creating the Mediterranean (meaning in Latin "between the lands") Sea. What is Asia moved south for centuries, then moved North and collided with Eastern Europe with such force that it created the Alps Mountain range between the two continents.

Over thousands of centuries the land mass was divided into several continents, each with different varieties of sunlight, temperature, plant and animal life, terrain, and germs. Then, over the next hundreds of centuries the human species originated in Central East Africa. Humans then spread to other parts of that continent, to the north, and to Europe and East Asia.

Over the next hundreds of centuries, some of her "descendants" roamed to other parts of Africa, and because of the climate, vegetation and animals, certain characteristics began to predominate, such as darker skin, a hairless face and body, and longer heads. Others wandered north to what we now know as Europe. There the colder climate, decreased sunlight, vegetation, and germs favored those with lighter skin, facial and body hair and a squarer face and head shape. If the migrant group becomes isolated due to the shift of land masses, it will continue to develop adaptive traits which will in time distinguish it very prominently from the group of which they were part before their migration and isolation.

Some migrants moved eastward over the Alps and over many thousands of years developed what came to be recognized as oriental features, such as: skin tone, rounded facial features, almond shaped eyes, and slight body build.

During the ice age, the sea level was well over 100 feet lower, so the land connection at the Bering Strait, which is between northeastern Russia and Alaska, was passable on foot. Thus, the American continents could be populated from origins in Africa. The low tide that allowed migrants from Africa to northeastern Europe to the Americas also made it possible for others to trek from southeast Asia to Australia.

Those who populated America became known as Indians because Amerigo Vespucci, an Italian Explorer, thought that he had sailed around the world to India. They formed about 300 tribes, many of whom fought one another. They became known as "red men" from the northwest. Much later, Caucasian, or "White men" from the east, some seeking treasure, but most to escape from oppression and privation of the ruling classes.

Some African tribes would war with one another. Those that won would take the others as captives. The English naval fleet would sail south to the west African coast, buy the captives for low value baubles and beads, sail them west to America for sale, then back northeast to England to enjoy their profits. The 3-way venture became known as the <u>golden triangle</u>. Thus, Black people helped to make Black slavery possible in America.

Trade ships from the U.S. to China often used the port of Shanghai. In the port there were vast numbers of Chinese men who were addicted to opium and were often doped up and defenseless. The U.S., seeing a need for cheap labor to assist with railroad construction, loaded many of those helpless men onto the ships.

Such men were poorly paid and so often forced to plant dynamite to make paths through the mountains. Many were then killed in the ensuing blast because they could not get out of the force from the explosion. Thus, the phrase, "Ain't got a China-man's chance" was coined.

Railroad tracks could not be inclined more than ten feet in a mile. Thus, tracks were laid around or through mountains.

In 1927, the U.S. Supreme Court held in the Gong Lum case, that a school district in Mississippi could deny a young Chinese girl the right to attend an all "White" public school. She didn't have a "Chinaman's chance."

*"Keep, ancient lands, your storied pomp. Give me your tired, your poor, your huddled masses yearning to breathe free. Send them, the homeless, tempest tossed to me. I lift my lamp beside the golden door." –Emma Lazarus*

The founding and formation of the U.S. is comparative to different gardens, each with a special vegetable, gathered and put in a pot, each with a particular nutritional value. They are gathered in one pot, heated, and stirred. Ezekiel saw the wheel.

"Keep, ancient lands, your storied pomp..."

14,000 years ago, the Ice Age caused the lower sea level to where migrating people traversed what is now known as the being Start from N.E. Europe to N.W. Alaska and spread throughout North and South America.

They won, in one way, but lost in another:

Donald Murray - Won admission to University of Maryland however- because it was in the state supreme court it was effective only in the state.

Lloyd Gains - Won admission to University of Missouri whose defense was: we will pay for his admission to a university in another state. Scotus said that would be effective only if you paid for all the students to attend outside Missouri. That was 1939 when lynching was prevalent. Gains disappeared from the view, even of his family for the rest of his life.

Ada Lois Sipuel - Won the fight to attend the university of Oklahoma and did so, graduating with honors in three years. However, in all his classes she was always seated behind a curtain marked "FOR COLORED." In other words, she was "equal," but separate.

Heman Marion Sweatt - Won all the way. For all.

# Chapter 2: Civility

As peoples continued to migrate and settle, there appeared among them individuals of extraordinary knowledge and power who were ambassadors of civility and technology. Through every culture there arose spiritual leadership that seemed to be strikingly similar in their role to reach into the spiritual realm and bring back something for their community. They seemed to appear from the sky, or heaven and were referred to as:

- Mystic
- Shaman
- Wiseman
- Sibyl
- Sage
- Seers
- Sorcerer
- Spiritualist
- Wizard
- Prophet
- Guru
- Medicine men
- Oracle
- Visionary
- Dervish

Mystic – Through contemplation and surrendering of him or herself, the mystic can unite with or be absorbed into a deity and gain knowledge that is unattainable through the intellect. Mysticism is recognized by Christianity, Islam, Judaism, and Hinduism.

Shaman – Through an altered state of consciousness, a shaman has access to and is influenced by spirits that some deem to be good, and some deem to be evil. They do so for the purposes of healing, prophesizing, divining and to act as the custodians of religious lore. Shamen is part of several indigenous north Asian and North American cultures.

Wisemen – In Zoroastrianism, practiced in ancient Persia, wisemen are masters of occult arts. They seem to appear at major turning points in human history. For instance, "Pliny records a crowd of them standing amid the smoke and ruins after the great temple of Artemis at Ephesus burned to the ground (circa 356 B.C.). These Magi announced that the great temple's destruction augured the (virgin) birth of Alexander the Great, who of course would go on to conquer the known world, be declared a god and die at the age of 33."[1] In the book of Genesis, Pharaoh called upon the magicians and wisemen to interpret his dream. However, it was Joseph who translated the dream & warmed him of impending famine. Wisemen are said to have appeared at a celebration given by Nero. Herod called for them to find the long-prophesized, newborn Messiah; and they did show up as visitors at the Messiah's birth.

Sibyl – For Ancient Greeks and Romans, a Sibyl was a woman seer who foretold events, while in a state of frenzy, under the control of a deity. The Sibyl prophetess type gained acceptance across various parts of Roman reach. And a Sibyl was said to have predicted Jesus. From first century BCE, this influence touched followers of polytheistic religions and monotheistic religions.[2]

Sage – In ancient Mesopotamia, sages were called the Apkallū, a group that existed before the great deluge.[3] In ancient Greek belief, sages were considered people who attained wisdom.

Seer – Nearly every African culture, had special individuals who foretold coming events of importance. Many times, those insights were seen in dreams. Those individuals were revered and believed to be prophets or seers. They had a prominent role in guiding the community into the future. Though the Torah frowned

---

[1] Opinion | Secret Lives of the Wise Men - The New York Times (nytimes.com)
[2] Sibyl and Sibylline Oracles (jewishvirtuallibrary.org)
[3] The Seven Sages of Ancient Greece: Wisdom & Impact (thecollector.com)

upon it, the Israelites were often noted as engaging with seers. This phenomenon was common among many people groups from Greek to Norse, to Celtic, Babylonian, etc.

Sorcerer – Sorcerers were believed to play a significant role in many cultures in Africa, Europe, the Middle East, and Asian cultures. In China, one could have encountered a woman shaman or a male sorcerer.

Spiritualist – an individual who would act as a medium between those in the physical realm and the metaphysical. Spiritualists were said to communicate with souls that departed from this life. Spiritualism was very popular in Europe and in America during the 1800s.

Wizard – As far back as 3000 BC Egyptian papyrus, tell stories of magicians or wizards. Some think of wizard and magicians as being similar. But in ancient times they were not synonymous. Wizards were thought of as wise men, enlightening people with philosophy. It wasn't until after around the middle 1500s that wizards came to be viewed the same as magicians.

Magicians today are portrayed as harmless trickster, slight-of-hand artists who entertain. They were once thought of as possessing special powers from malevolent sources. Both magicians and wizards are said to work with demons. And these concepts were found in various cultures.

Prophet – Prophets have been known to be a part of many cultures and religions throughout history, including Judaism, Christianity, Islam, ancient Greek religion, Zoroastrianism, Manichaeism, Hinduism, and many others. A prophet or a prophetess is an individual who is thought to be in contact with a divine being and it speaks on behalf of that being, serving as an intermediary with humanity by delivering messages or teachings from that supernatural source. Many people are familiar with the prophets of the Abrahamic religions, but there were also prophets in ancient Mesopotamia, Egypt, and Greece. They existed also among early Buddhists in China and Tibet, the indigenous peoples of the Americas, Europeans, and continue today.

Guru – Guru is a Sanskrit word for a reverenced, spiritual teacher, especially one who imparts initiation. In ancient India, in Hinduism, knowledge of the Vedas (spiritual literature) was taught orally from guru to pupil. Gurus were the living embodiments of spiritual truth and were identified with a personal deity. Gurus prescribe spiritual disciplines to their devotees, who follow their dictates in a tradition of service and obedience. Buddhism began in India in the fifth century[4] and spread into China, Taiwan, Japan, South Korea, Cambodia, Thailand, Burma (Myanmar), Bhutan, Sri Lanka, Laos, and Mongolia. In the Tibetan tradition, the guru is seen as The Buddha, the very root of Spiritual realization and the basis of the path.

Medicine Man – A person, especially among Indigenous American groups who is believed to possess supernatural powers to heal the sick and to keep away evil spirits. Also known as a shaman or priest, the medicine person (male or female) operates in the spiritual world and is a spiritual guide.[5]

Oracle – (700 B.C. - A.D. 300) The oracles of Greece and the sibyls of Rome were women chosen by the gods through which divine advice would be spoken through them. They were popular throughout the great empires and pilgrims would make their way from far off places just to ask them a question and receive the answer of a god.[6] For example, the God of the Sun was an oracle.

Visionary – All ancient societies had visionaries. They were connected to the universal source consciousness and pass on insights from the spirit world. Visionaries serve as a reflection of

---

[4] https://news.stanford.edu/2018/08/20/stanford-scholar-discusses-buddhism-origins/
[5] https://www.nature.com/articles/138268b0
[6] https://departments.kings.edu/womens_history/ancoracles.html

your own spiritual practice, reminding one that they already have the answers within themselves.[7]

Dervish – A Sufi religious order who has taken vows of poverty and austerity. Dervishes were spiritual initiates who first appeared in the 12th century; they were noted for their wild or ecstatic rituals and were known as dancing, whirling, or howling dervishes according to the practice of their order. Mevlevis are also known as the "whirling dervishes" because of their famous practice of whirling as a way of remembering God. Whirling is part of the formal sema ceremony.[8]

These people hold a unique and revered place in the cultures where they existed (and exist today). Some believe that they have abilities that go beyond the commonplace; and that their knowledge may even be considered other-worldly. Could they have been influenced by a higher understanding that does not yet exist here?

Individuals of higher knowledge have, through observation, recognized what is needed in our world. Even with their in-depth understanding, they are careful to be inclusive and not exclusive. They are respectful of fellow human beings and have no inkling of superiority in their manner. They present themselves as examples that we can model ourselves after, for our own betterment and for the improvement of the human condition. This is the epitome of civility.

It is axiomatic that no one of us created the circumstances into which we were born. Not the signs and symbols, nor the prides, passion or processes which were moving along apace, and certainly not the perceptions by which we are viewed by those surrounding us. Family, ethnicity, intimate community, religious traditions, and social orders all embody values and ideals which

---

[7] https://www.sheilaprycebrooks.com/wp-content/uploads/2022/08/Visionary-Spiritual-Experiences-in-an-Enchanted-World.pdf
[8] https://istanbuldervishceremony.com/what-is-a-whirling-dervish-and-why-is-it-called-that/

may range from self-serving ego to world serving brotherhood and unity.

Countless human dramas are played out as individuals either accept the limitations and requirements of the extant powers and thereby reinforce the system, or somehow draw upon the inner creative powers with which they have been endowed to gain a new vision of who they are and why they exist, and thereby reshape the course of events. Of such is the substance of history. In a word, we are a part of the process we are studying.

Communication is not so much a matter of transmitting ideas, as stimulating memories of past experiences. For example, words, signs, as well as everything that is being experienced at any given point in time, goes into the memory bank. This can cause confusion/distortion as the same concept recurs in a variety of settings until circumspect is gained. Associations are made, and a new experience may, thus, broaden experience base. At some level, would-be communicators know this, yet they continue to try to "transmit" through the "static." Logically, then, the narrower the experience base, the more difficult will be communication, for the sender and for the receiver. Also, the more emotion there is, the more likely there is a broad experience base of memory. However, as in dreams, there is a greater chance of distortion.

Experiences are inner and outer. The memory makes little distinction. Distortion comes when one wants experience to have a particular meaning, as when a politician tries to advocate certain ideals without first obtaining a consensus with reference to an idea. This may explain why "truth" has a "ring" to it, like a note sounded on one instrument creates a vibration, which stimulates a string on another instrument to vibrate in sympathy. Does this ring true to you? This illustration "communicates" to those whose experiences include musical stringed instruments but remains vague to others.

Perhaps the Native American ways of slow familiarity have great merit. Words are like shadows, which cast a mishappened

10

image of an idea: the receiver must give it form and substance from their experience base, and/imagination.

Looking at history as a litany of facts, statistics, catastrophes, and triumphs without taking into account the ultimate purpose of mankind is like looking at a series of black and white photographs. But now we can, and indeed are impelled, to look at the continuum of human experience as a motion picture in full Technicolor and 3-D. What is more, you are in the picture. There is no more "we" vs "they. Even in war it is now "we against us, ourselves". As Pogo says, "we have found the enemy…he is us."

The existential moment – when by the choices we make in this pivotal decade we get to know who we are, perhaps the highest goal in life. Now several questions arise, and you can show your shape. How will you use your position, powers, and capacities to bring about greater unity to deal with the ills that afflict mankind? Just as the right hand washes the left; the left hand does not escape washing the right hand. All of us resulted from a fusion of sperm & egg. These cells are too tiny to see & yet they contain within them all the qualities needed to form a fully functioning human being. Within us is the power & wisdom to develop a brain, a heart, lungs, skin, etc. They work together perfectly but, many times we use it to separate ourselves. As these structures develop, they have no relation to anything else; they form their own capacity. Then comes a point of decision; that is where they agree to cooperate. The body parts become inter-dependent. When the parts don't agree we have a malady. Mankind is going through this right now… deciding if we will be interdependent. Who are your allies? Will you realize your full potential as a unique creation? Will you adorn the pages of future histories?

This era has been called the Aquarian Age when people accomplished deeds by working in groups. and there was an increase in harmony in the world. The various nations and tribes of the earth are like different gardens of fruits and vegetables, each with its one nutritious specialty. Each group has its own identifying motif. Yet, strangely, everyone does not conform precisely to the expected ideology of their group, but indeed, may be closely associated with many groups.

There is a compelling analogy between an organically related society and a healthy human body. A general multilateral acceptance of cultural strengths and the sacrifices each has had to make to develop their qualities are necessary for world peace and unity. Each person must have some concept of the purpose of the whole and his place in it. This is based the premise that each of the identifiable races, nations, and cultures of the world displays a particular attribute or attributes of God. These attributes can be viewed as necessary for world unity, and for the solution of problems which beset peoples. We can view the tribulations of each group with new understanding, appreciation, and compassion, and resolve to vindicate their sufferings. Think of how qualities that we normally associate with a particular group or culture would help alleviate a particular ill of humanity if only representatives of each group could come to consult freely and openly about his experiences and understandings and as members of each group co-mingle and interrelate.

Just as the gardener cultivates his fields separately and harvests his orchards together for a well-rounded meal which nourishes the entire body, so the spiritual qualities have been cultivated, are being harvested and prepared to nourish the spiritual needs of mankind.

# Chapter 3: Power

From the beginnings of civility peoples have been controlled by those few who had power, the fist, the spear, bow and arrows, guns, armies, bombs, and now money and corporate wealth. Today, that power determines the outbreak and/or outcome of international war.

In all human institutions throughout the past whether family, clan, village, tribe, city, state or nation, a relatively small number manage, whether by threat or force, of arms, wealth, religious persuasion or dominance, gain power, that is the authority to impose an identity on all the members and control the fortune and destiny of all under their authority.

During the last century a new power began to manifest itself. It is wielded by the New Race of Men as they emerge from the ranks of the general population of mankind, including members of all colors, cultures, and customs. They are being summoned forth by the patent immaturity of the current administration and are bonded together by the spirit of unity and brotherhood.

The Bahá'í community is inclusive. It encompasses a variety of people from various religious origins. Bahá'í ideals have been taught from the very beginning. In life, there is one school for humanity; but just like in the school system, there are several grades. Just as in early learning, we first learn the characters of the alphabet. Once, we've mastered the alphabet we can form words. We learn to use our words to then construct sentences to transfer our thoughts. In the time of Abraham, we were about the equivalent of the first grade. Move on to Moses' time and we used our first-grade knowledge to understand the second grade, and progress onward. As we evolved to paragraphs, chapters and beyond, each example represents a new teacher and a deeper understanding. Each time, the teacher said, 'I will come again unto you' or 'another will come to you'. When Messiah was among the Hebrews, some of them challenged him & said he was against Moses. He said 'If you had believed Moses then you would have believed me, for he wrote of me' I cannot go against Moses. At the time of Moses (many generations before) Moses led the people from captivity to the promised land. Before He passed away it was said to Moses from heaven, I will raise up one like unto yourself, from among your people. The Messiah was that one.

It was not a different religion. It was a different grade level.

Why would the Almighty send someone to teach – then send another to tell everyone to forget all of that – of course He didn't. Remember what Moses taught you. Use that to further your insight I will return to elevate you more.

In visiting many churches and synagogues, for years, it is noted that we are all in the same school – just in different grades. No matter what your belief system: Abraham, Moses, Zeus, Zoroaster, or another; we are all seeking to develop and grow. Mankind cannot get away from this. We try by going to war with brothers and sisters rather than to try and understand, that we are only one race. Some are growing. Some are not growing.

In the Bahá'í faith, the motivation and purpose are to erase tension, find points of agreement and to help each other embrace a higher level of understanding. Mankind MUST come together, otherwise we will all suffer and contend against one another. Many people are striving to improve the spiritual condition of mankind. They may not be the largest percentage of people, but their numbers are not small.

Professor A.P. Watson, Sr. was a college professor and very active in race relations in the community. Professor Watson and this anonymous teacher did not know one another prior to this meeting. They had instant fellowship at this juncture. His new friend (also a teacher) was restricted from teaching anything positive about Black people. So, his friend invested in converting a bus to be a moving classroom to teach Black history. He became a target. Professor Watson was the only person willing to host this teacher. His name was kept private to protect him.

Some people are so insecure that they feel it necessary to denigrate others. We can't change things by force. It must be by cooperation.

As previously noted, other cultures and races have had many similar experiences... Commentator Clarence Page, referring to the award-winning movie "Crash" writes, "It surprises us with characters whose inner natures contradict their outer appearance, good or evil, making them as complicated and inexplicable as people we know in real life." The movie "presents inter-group conflicts in a way you seldom see on the news as outer expressions of inner personal pain.

Whether deliberately or inadvertently, certain institutions in our society (such as family, religious order, schools, political or social subgroups), "teach" us who we are, and whom "they" are, referring to those people outside our referenced group. We also learn how to treat "them" and what can be expected of "them", as well as what to expect from each other. Stereotypes facilitate decision-making but inhibit understanding.

# Chapter 4: The Constitution

The United States Constitution is a sterling example of a wise and thoughtful document. It is one that espouses many of the ideals of cooperation and respect for humanity. However, it is not flawless. For instance, in Article One it states that any person who was not free would be counted as <u>three-fifths</u> of a free individual. It's also important to note that, it represented high ideals that were memorialized on paper, and blatantly ignored in practice. The reality is that, for Native Americans and African Americans, those ideals were seldom honored in American life. People of Color were not the image the framers held in their minds when they said: "All men are created equal." They were not considered when the writers wrote: "… with liberty and justice for all."

However, native peoples were a part of the development of the US constitution. Native societies were already governing themselves in a democratic way. While displaced Europeans were fighting the American Revolution and designing this highly regarded document, many "American" natives in the Haudenosaunee Confederacy (for example) had already been living an oral constitution called "The Great Law of Peace". The democracy of the native people had been thriving since at least 1142. It included separation of powers, it had provisions for impeachment and was based on the ideals of liberty, unity, and equality.[9]

## 14<u>th</u> Amendment

In 1868 the Fourteenth Amendment of the US Constitution was ratified. It granted five major provisions; namely that:

1. All persons born or naturalized in the US, including the former enslaved, were granted citizenship in the United States and the state in which they reside. It went on to also say that no state is allowed to abridge the privileges or immunities of US citizens; neither is a state allowed to deprive any person of life, liberty, or

---

[9] https://www.discovermagazine.com/planet-earth/did-native-americans-shape-u-s-democracy

property, without due process; nor deny any person equal protection under the laws.

2. Each state shall receive representation according to their number of citizens (excluding Native Americans who are not taxed); however, if the right to vote is denied to any adult male citizen (except for rebellion, or crime) then the representation shall be reduced in proportion.

3. No one who has taken an oath to represent the People in Congress, as President or Vice-President, or hold office in the US government or State government, shall engage in insurrection or rebellion against the government. Congress may with a vote of two-thirds of each house, remove such.

4. Neither the United States government nor any State government shall pay any debt incurred in aid of insurrection against the US; neither shall the government pay any loss associated with emancipation of any slave.

5. Congress shall have the power to enforce the provisions of this Article.

All states had to ratify this Amendment in order to have federal representation. The Civil Rights Act of 1964 and the Voting Rights Act of 1965 were made possible by the Fourteenth Amendment.

The three-fifths compromise was negated or cancelled by the statement that 'All persons born or naturalized in the US, including the former enslaved, were granted citizenship in the United States and the state in which they reside.'; along with the declaration that the government is not allowed to be allowed to abridge or deny the rights of its citizens without due process'.

The wording in this article is unclear! Perhaps it is deliberately so. However, once again, the written representation of America did not play out in the lives of its people.

This is the 14<sup>th</sup> Amendment of the United States Constitution. Separate but equal is a phrase first coined by the Supreme Court of the United States (SCOTUS) in the Plessy v. Ferguson Landmark case (1896) which gave legitimacy to the state and local laws which imposed an identity on citizens for purposes of granting privileges or sanctions. In the Plessy case, a fair com-plexioned man, a passenger on a train went to the dining car to be served. Despite his protests he was denied service and put off the train.

In 1896, SCOTUS ruled that a facility that served the public may discriminate against a person based on racial identity on the condition that they provide equal service at a separate place. That ruling resulted in sub-standard facilities and services provided for a people who were perceived as being a lower rank of humans. This warped view was held by the general public, who had lost sight of the knowledge that there is but one race of human beings. That sentiment also tended to perpetuate itself by the very separation that it imposed. This acculturation was promoted openly and subtly by respected institutions, especially public schools. Whether the media, schools, churches, synagogue, temples, or mosques admit it or not, they "taught" society to think of Black people as "other". That conditioning created a pseudo-reality in the mind, like hovering shadows that dull the thinking. They do not "unlearn" these precepts any more than we unlearn anything. But they can learn more, which can change entirely the import of what they knew before. They are oriented towards each other like keys on the piano. A pianist could not play a charming piece, deftly skipping along the keys, without the benefit of orientation provided by the black and white keys. Each distinct people demand morals, produce art, and become a color-rich chord in a grand symphony.

# Chapter 5: Cycle of Oppression

The cycle of racial Conditioning:

1. **Prepare the perpetrators to mistreat the victims targeted by racism:**

   - Hurt and disempower the perpetrators when they are children and instill patterns of hopelessness, powerlessness, and an unconscious compulsion to reenact their abuse on those they perceive as less powerful than themselves.
   - Give the perpetrators gross misinformation about the group that you wish them to target for mistreatment while at the same time withholding accurate information about the history of the perpetrators' group and the targeted group.
   - Keep the perpetrators separate from the victims so the perpetrators cannot discover the inherent humanity of the victim.

2. **The perpetrators acting out of their own racial conditioning perpetuate institutionalized injustice on racism's victims.**

3. **The victims of racism internalize the mistreatment and misinformation and then act it out on each other.**

   - The targeted group, having been mistreated over the long period of time, internalizes the mistreatment and the misinformation about themselves and their group and comes to believe, consciously or unconsciously, the racist stereotypes that are perpetuated in the nation in which they live.

- The victims, having internalized the racist misinformation and hurtful behavior, then perpetuate the same mistreatment and misinformation on themselves, their family, and those closest to them.

4. **The perpetrators use the internalized oppression of the victims to justify further mistreatment of the targeted group.**

# Chapter 6: Black Like Me

After the World War 2, there were writers who wanted to depict life in particular countries: "Inside Russia or inside Egypt". J. Howard Griffin was so overtaken by the animosity and atrocities in this country that he wanted to write about life <u>Inside America</u>. He wanted to write from firsthand experiences. To do so, he had his skin darkened and hair modified. As sophisticated as he was, he was over-taken by ordinary experiences of being Black in America. For a short time, he walked through the world as a Black worker. He discovered he would have to be very careful with even the most common day-to-day activities. Where could he use the bathroom? Where could he get a meal without the threat of losing his life? He chose to title his book, "Black Like Me."

# Chapter 7: Lynching

W.E.B. Dubois wrote, "One ever feels his two-ness, - an American, and a negro, two souls, two thoughts, two unrecognized strivings, and two warring ideals in one dark body. The history of the American Negro is the history of this strife; this longing to merge his double self, in to a better and truer self. In this merging he wishes neither of the older selves to be lost." The same can be said of Latinos, Native people, and Asians. Many Caucasians are also caught in the paradox with minds torn by love-hate thoughts, i.e.: 'I have been taught to hate, dislike or distrust "others", yet I admire the capacities of some of "them".'

The author, Ida B. Wells-Barnett, writing in a 1900 article titled "Lynch Law in America," has the following: "Not only are two hundred men and women put to death annually, on the average, in this country by mobs, but these lives are taken with the greatest publicity… Whenever a burning is advertised to take place, the railroads run excursions, photographs are taken, and the same jubilee is indulged in that characterized the public hangings of one hundred years ago. There is however, this difference: in the old days the multitude that stood by was permitted only to guy or jeer. The nineteenth century lynching mobs cut off ears, toes, fingers, and strips of flesh, and then distributes portions of the body as souvenirs among the crowd. If the leaders of the mob are so minded, coal-oil is poured over the body and the victim is roasted to death.

So many people that call themselves liberty loving Americans try to assert a sense of superiority. Thousands of 'outstanding citizens' lynched other 'outstanding citizens' because their skin tone was different than their own. Countless scientific inventions are held up in pride. But the originators of so many of those products were Black inventors; and those facts have been hidden.

# Chapter 8: Two Movements

Niagara

During the early nineteen hundreds there were some elite persons who were deeply concerned about the racial injustice and atrocities in this country. They chose to meet to make plans to effectuate legal changes in northern New York and Southern Canada. In the city of Niagara, they had the understanding that one-tenth of the Black citizens had special talents and referred to them as the "Talented Tenth".

The resulting organization became known as the National Association for the Advancement of Colored People, **"NAACP"**, in 1909. This became known as the **Niagara Movement**. Their main thrust was to change laws which supported racial segregation. "**Charles Hamilton Houston** was one of the pioneers: After becoming the first African American on the Harvard Law Review, he became dean of the law school at all-Black Howard University. Stern and uncompromising, Houston soon earned the nickname" Old Iron shoes." But he transformed a third-rate night school into a West Pointe for civil rights advocacy.

One of Houston's students was a brash young man from Baltimore named Thurgood Marshall. Soon after Marshall graduated from Howard. Houston and his former student took charge of the NAACP'S legal office. The abstemious, proper Houston and the folksy, easygoing Marshall made an unlikely duo, but together they faced down angry southern mobs, negotiated with presidents and senators, and convinced even the most racist judges and juries that the Constitution demanded equal justice under the law for all Americans. Case by case, precedent by precedent they undermined the legal foundations of Jim Crow.

After graduating from Howard University, Thurgood Marshall applied to the University of Maryland Law School and was denied. In 1936, another qualified African American applied to the University of Maryland Law School. Upon being denied, the

NAACP took the case to the Maryland Supreme Court and won entry. However, this was effective only in the state of Maryland.

Houston, tragically, would die before his strategy came to fruition in Brown, but Marshall would argue the case victoriously, going on to become the first African American Supreme Court justice- always crediting his mentor for his success. Together, the two men changed the course of American history.

The Niagara Movement was founded in 1905 by WEB DuBois and William Monroe Trotter. What made them successful? They located themselves near the Canada border for smaller chance of apprehension. They carefully developed a winning strategy (schools they could open, jobs, positions). In the Black community they had something called the 'talented tenth'. Someone had the idea that one tenth of the Black community, in its current state (at the time), could readily advance beyond cotton picking. They would be better prepared than their White counterparts to move the vision forward. They would be the ranks of people that would be fortified with the plans & strategies necessary to advance America a little further toward the ideals that it ascribes to in its rhetoric.

### Gaines V. Missouri

In 1938, the NAACP took the case of Lloyd Gaines and won him admission to the University of Missouri. The state of Missouri said that they would be willing to pay his tuition in any law school, outside the state of Missouri. The U.S Supreme Court said that the argument would be acceptable only if they would pay the tuition of every student outside the state. This significant win for the NAACP was compounded when Lloyd Gaines would not show up to enter law school. He disappeared and could not be found. The public can only speculate as to why he disappeared. It could be reasoned that since any Negro person that was in the public eye was a target for lynching, he was deterred from the challenge.

This was a win, but it did not produce any traction. It did not advance integration.

## Oklahoma – Ada Louis Sipuel

"A matter of Black and White", is the personal story of an Oklahoma woman whose fight to gain education formed a crucial episode in the civil rights movement. Born in Chikasha, Oklahoma whose parents were only one generation removed from slavery, Ada Lois Sipuel Fisher, became the plaintiff in a Landmark U.S Supreme Court case that laid the foundation for eventual desegregation of schools (and much else) in America. When Oklahoma gained statehood in 1907, the first bill passed by the Legislature called for segregation of the state's public schools and universities. No one successfully challenged segregation until 1946, when Ada Sipuel, a recent graduate of an all- Black Langston University, applied for admission to the all-White University of Oklahoma Law School. Because Oklahoma had no segregation law for Blacks, she argued, the state's official policy of "separate but equal" education was illusory. Her simple act of applying to a White law school touched off a fire storm of controversy. At its center was a fierce legal battle waged by NAACP lawyers, including Thurgood Marshall. Fisher's autobiography reflects much of the history of American Blacks and Whites and of changing relationships through this century. It is also the history of family and community life in a small southern town during years of legal segregation, racial discrimination, and economic depression. The people of this remarkable family community did more than endure in trying times, they triumphed. She applied in Oklahoma in 1946, the same year Heman Sweatt applied in Texas. Her case was won in the Supreme Court in 1948. The law school stipulated that she must sit behind a curtain marked "for colored," she and the negro community finally acceded to that. Why then did the NAACP still have to pursue the Sweatt case?

But this did not break down segregation. This was an example of separate but un-equal.

When Wiley College was at the center of attention, Thurgood Marshall teamed up with Charles Hamilton Houston. Houston was the lead counsel & a professor at Howard University. Marshall was once his student. Marshall could be a little brash at times. Hamilton had a more modest temperament, but superior legal skills. Thurgood had a fiery personality and people considered him more direct.

When he was being considered for Supreme Court, he acknowledged that Houston would have been the first choice. But when Houston passed away, Marshall became the preference.

# Chapter 9: What keeps us APART

Appearance – the obvious element, that makes it simple to identify an established 'enemy'. However, here is an example of how appearance can pull people together. Brande was drafted in the army, in 1954 – Truman desegregated the army, but only a few privates were in his company. He volunteered to be a paratrooper. He had to pass physical tests to be accepted as a paratrooper. Different companies were accumulated. Brande was standing with his company – another White soldier (kind of small) was standing nearby and started talking to Brande. They called him Yocum. He talked as though he and Brande had been long established friends. Brande tall and African American and Yocum small in stature and Caucasian, made quite the sight. Yocum wanted to team up with Brande to pass the paratrooper exam. Yocum helped Brande make his 20 pullups. For sit-ups, they would hold each other's ankles. The Sargent who was keeping count, got the points from the person holding the other soldier's ankles. Unprompted, when Yocum noticed Brande starting to struggle in the sit-ups, he practiced creative counting. He reported the total 50 sit-ups (and counted in this way: 23, 24, 25, 36, 37, 38, 49). His counting was a signal to Brande, that 'hey, I'm with you'.

Years after returning home from the army, Brande was driving a motorcycle, in southeast Texas. He lost his way & saw a sign for Yocum, TX! That was when Brande realized that Yocum was not the actual name of that soldier. It was his hometown – the same place made famous by Lil'Abner (the main character in a satirical comic strip that ran from 1934 until 1977).

When we observe these examples of raw racism instigating itself into the lives of people and causing unrelenting trauma, we must ask ourselves, 'Why?' When we witness these unprovoked and unjustified horrors and their enduring impact that dribbles down into successive generations, we are forced to wonder, 'How can we make it stop?'

Over the course of centuries, creative minds have attempted various strategies to foster cooperation. All this ingenuity was somehow manifested while under insurmountable duress. How can the exploited prey dissuade their aggressors from perpetuating more suffering. They were not in a position of power, but of servitude. Black civil rights leaders and White passivists have dug deep to unlock the secret solution to ending the man-made illusion of race. So far, this has been to no avail and many times the peacemakers ended as martyrs.

Yes, the Creator made man in a multitude of heights, widths, shades, and other differentiating characteristics. None of these distinguishing factors makes anyone innately superior or inferior. Eventually, Caucasians will be forced to recognize that insane cruelty, visited upon those who are the object of their fixation, is an exercise in insanity. Introspection will make it clear that one's inability to produce melanin is not justification for effecting needless brutality on those who can. Perhaps it is our differences that will ultimately prove to us that we are amazingly similar. One day we will discern that there is only one race of people on earth – the humankind.

**P**ossessions – Another simplistic but effective means of separating people, is to segment them according to their economic status. Said another way, how much 'Stuff' can they acquire and at what level of extravagance? America presents several layers of illusions to cover inequalities. The myth of meritocracy says that any American can pull his or herself up by the bootstraps. But tell that to the child born in a broken-down ghetto, with inferior schools, tired teachers, outdated books, living in a literal food desert with no access to nutrition, no exposure to a better life, walking to school in a war zone. See if they can imagine a life that their parents never saw, despite their dedicated work ethic. A place where loans are withheld or assessed higher interest rates based on their neighborhood or literal skin color. An environment where the amount of income is always outpaced by the cost of living.

Meanwhile, the privileged grow their inheritances on the backs of the descendants of slaves. Business Insider shows that, in 2022, the average, middle-class White family had a $984K net worth as compared to $188K net worth of the average, middle-class Black family. Clearly, "White families hold more than five times the wealth of the typical Black family and more than four times the wealth of the typical Hispanic family."[10]

All of this becomes evident in the neighborhoods that these families can afford to live in. It shows in the quality of home they can acquire. It is obvious by observing the type, quantity, and quality of possessions for the average families across the demographic spectrum, that race plays an important part in quality of life.

**A**chievements – As go educational opportunities, and thereby earning potential; there follows the achievement gap. The data shows that factors like **race, income, and zip code have a bigger impact on health than behavior, medical care, or genetic code.** These social determinants of health are also social determinants of economic and social class mobility–those that get good educations are more likely to earn more and achieve positions of authority, those that earn more are able to take advantage of more opportunities and experiences, and those who hold positions of power are able to make decisions that benefit them and their families. Great disparities exist between White and non-White people in education, money, and the concentration of power, which gives White people a significant advantage in achieving and maintaining good health.[11]

**R**elationships – Healthy relationships are composed of healthy individuals who can bring enough of themselves to the equation.

**T**alk – The best resolution for division is to communicate, open up understanding, and build consensus. Going back to the inter-

---

[10] https://www.bankrate.com/banking/savings/savings-account-average-balance/
[11] https://centerforhealthprogress.org/blog/publications/health-white-privilege/

dependency of the embryonic cells that must learn to cooperate to survive; those cells must communicate. There is an entire system of communication, within each of us, that is required for survival. We, as microcosms, reflect the reality of the macrocosm of mankind. We must cooperate, and hold each other in equal esteem, in order continue as a species. Not one of us is superior to another. Not one of us is inferior. We each have a role to play in the grand design.

# Chapter 10: Race Amity Movement

The public mindset needed an overhaul. Beginning in 1912, and continuing for several decades thereafter; a young man named Louis Gregory culled from the ranks of religious, social, and humanitarian organizations citizens of many backgrounds and heritages to augur for fairness. A young Afro-American lawyer, Louis Gregory was a lynchpin of that movement. He, himself, was in an interracial marriage. Together with Agnes Parsons, a White socialite who lived in Washington D.C., and a fellow member of the Bahá'í Faith, he worked on race amity conferences.

The Bahá'í Faith is a religion which holds as a basic principle the oneness and wholeness of the human race. The American Bahá'í seeks to establish race amity. Its administrative headquarters in America began in 1909, very close in time and place of the Niagara Movement, which later became the NAACP. The movement was highly esteemed and functioned in many cities throughout the country, even at the time when lynchings and other atrocities rankled and horrified the country.

Louis Gregory's story presents a rich tapestry that invites deep and thoughtful study. He was a lawyer, one of the talented tenth, yet he gave up a promising career to devote his energies full-time to spreading the teachings of the Bahá'í Faith … throughout the United States. He knew and associated with virtually all the Black leaders of his day, educators, clergyman, heads of civil rights organizations and many leading Whites as well. Noble-minded, golden hearted, he was widely known as a lecturer and writer for racial unity… He stood in the forefront of every struggle. It was said of Louis Gregory: "Now some men falter when they perceive the summons of a divine truth. And some men hesitate or delay the moment of complete dedication fearing its price. But others, as soon as they have found the highest altar of life, lay all that they are and have upon that altar with a love that banishes reluctance and fear. Such a man was Louis Gregory." Elsie Austin

A report in the Bahá'í News described Louis Gregory's highly successful visit to Houston Texas in 1944. Besides a series of advertised public meetings attended by 75 to 150 people of both races there were several fireside meetings and dinner parties. The secretary of the Houston Assembly wrote that she had never witnessed such a clamoring for Bahá'í literature and for the opportunity to hear a Bahá'í speaker. The people who attended brought friends and sat at the feet of Louis Gregory. Many public meeting places were found where there was no segregation of races and meetings were held in the Negro districts, with no objections whatsoever on the part of the White inquirers. Both Negro and White business and professional men attended these meetings as well as lieutenants and sergeants from the military base of Ellington Field.

# Chapter 11: A Consequential Sequence

Wiley, a historically Black college was founded in 1873 in a small town of Marshall in East Texas. It became accredited in 1933. Perhaps the most significant factor in that accreditation was the debate team, coached by Professor Melvin Tolson, which won 73 of 74 debates including contentions with the most prestigious universities in the country.

James Sweatt, Heman Sweatt's father, was a forceful man of great dignity who set an example of social activism, for his children to follow. A graduate from Prairie View College in Texas, he worked as a teacher and principal in Beaumont, Texas, and later as a railway mail clerk in Houston. He helped organize other clerks to oppose the "Caucasian Clause" of Mutual Benefit Association which barred the issuance of insurance policies to Black clerks. He was a charter member of the NAACP branch and a member of the African Methodist Episcopal Church.

The older of his six children went to colleges out of the state of Texas. A younger son, Heman, chose to attend Wiley College and major in biology, his intentions to become a medical doctor.

Sweatt studied under James H. Morton, who later became President of the Austin NAACP branch. His most inspiring teacher, however, was Melvin B. Tolson, poet laureate of Liberia and acclaimed author of *Harlem Gallery.* Tolson was an eloquent orator and a powerful voice when speaking against racial discrimination, and Sweatt later acknowledged him as a major influence on his life.

Wiley College located in northeast Texas, was the first baccalaureate institution for Black students west of the Mississippi to be certified. That was accomplished in large measure due to the phenomenal successes of the debate team in defeating some of the most distinguished universities in the country. The coach of that team was Professor M.B. Tolson.

Nolan Anderson was a fellow student and biology major with Heman Sweatt. Both were members of the debate team.

## A Grain of Sand

**Nolan:** Let's go debate with Tolson and dissect some arguments. Professor Tolson's an enigmatic and colorful teacher of English, a poet, writer, playwright, and activist, and most notably, the coach of the debate team. He is their favorite faculty member.

**Heman:** I want to go to med school, but Tolson gets under my skin... so to speak.

**Nolan:** Well, this is a language lab...

The college classroom debate team is being coached by Prof. Tolson; it is made up of 12 students including Heman and Nolan.

**Nolan:** Prof. Tolson picks apart your thoughts like we dissect a frog in the lab. He triggers your thoughts with elocution like: "Democracy is a form of government in which it is permitted to wonder aloud what the country could do under first class management.

**Student:** "Who said that?"

**Prof Tolson:** "Senator Soaper. Now be a master of your petty annoyances and conserve your energies for worthwhile things. It isn't the mountain ahead that wears you out; it's the grain of sand in your shoe."

**Heman:** How does he remember all this?

**Nolan:** He started young ... and he doesn't sleep.

**Heman:** He also seems to write a lot.

**Student:** He writes and directs plays. I'm in his English class, and if you're not clear you're going to get a lecture.

**Prof Tolsson:** "Sally forth into the arena of debate. Suffer not the benign neglect of the expectators, benumbed and impeached by the grand sweep of it all. Do not dally in indecision-outdistance past celebrity and rewire its fortunes."

Tolson's drama productions, and even more his coaching of the phenomenally successful Wily College debate team, made him an iconoclast of conventional teaching methods who set a new spin to the hopes, aspirations, and even self-images of so many of his students and admirers. Heman and a classmate, Noland Anderson became fast friends and participants on the debate team.

Heman Sweatt

In Marshall, Texas, 1948. Heman visits the home of Prof. A.P. Watson Sr., professor at Wiley College, his wife and three sons, ages 16, 15, and 11. Watson is chairman of the East Texas chapter of NAACP, very active and supportive of Heman. (Heman's favorite teacher, Prof. Tolson, left Wiley in 1947.) Heman stayed to have dinner with the Watson family. Lively discussion was had.

**Prof Watson:** For instance, in '39 I went to Dallas when friends told me that White thugs were riding the streets, shooting. I took one of my sons with me. My host wanted me to let my son (Brande) sleep behind the couch out of sight in case of another incident.

**Prof Watson:** We don't know who's with us or against us. Sometimes we think we're falling into their arms only to find that we're falling into their hands. They do a pirouette. Some Whites help; some Negros betray us. We are not able to see through each other, but to see each other through.

**Heman:** I think a lot like you.

**Prof Watson:** Tolson had to…rather was forced to leave Wiley. He went to Langston, Oklahoma. It wasn't just "downtown", but here on campus. A secret is what you tell one person at a time. (Laughter) Man's capacity for justice makes democracy possible. Man's capacity for injustice makes democracy necessary. The greatest influence on history has been historians. For instance, not much has been written about the Black battalion that took San Quan Hill for Teddy Roosevelt's army; And how he wanted to commend them highly. Chroniclers just let it be assumed that it was his usual regiment.

**Heman:** I wish you had been here to teach history when I was here. I would have enjoyed your classes. I graduated in '34, the year before you came to Wiley.

After Heman filed suit against UT Law School, he and his wife were under serious violent threat by White mobsters.

A Barbershop Quartet

In a Houston barbershop, 10 0r 12 "Black" males, in a somewhat raucous discussion about the threats on Heman Sweatt's life, and what they would do if he were hurt.

**Man:** I f they hurt that man, we gonna have war in the U.S of A

**Man 1:** Lord be my helper, I ain't just gonna stand by....

**Man2:** The police ain't gon help!

**Man3:** I don't hesitate to relate that at this date, we should retaliate and not just cogitate.

**Man4:** What school did you drop out of, old son?

**Man1:** I fought the Nazis in Sicily and France, and I'll fight these throwbacks here.

**Man3:** I got my gun, and I'll guard his house every night.

**Man1:** If they keep this up, I'm for getting even.

**Man 4:** The greatest odds are against getting even.

Heman graduated from Wiley in 1934; the year after Wiley College received its "A" rating thus he graduated from an accredited college. After graduating Sweatt pursued a variety of occupations. He worked as a porter, then as a teacher, and finally entered graduate school in public health at the University of Michigan. The harsh winters in Michigan, however, kept Sweatt poor health and he ultimately returned to Houston, where he found work in the post office. At the time that he decided to apply to law school at the University of Texas, Heman Sweatt had been employed at the post office for a considerable time, owned a house in Houston, and had been involved in the NAACP for many years. He had befriended prominent activists like Lulu White, the mainstay of the Houston NAACP chapter. He was acquainted with the other plaintiffs in anti-discrimination litigation, and he helped to raise funds for lawsuits against all-White primaries and participated in the voter registration drives. He was, in essence, very prepared to battle racial discrimination.

Notably, however he met, at University of Michigan, Lloyd Gaines, a Negro who had been the lead man in the NAACP suit against the University of Missouri, which was decided in 1938. Gaines had a raucous temperament, diametrically opposite of

Sweatt. The question arises, why that case did not end the quest for the overturn of separate but equal doctrine in the nation's school system; a doctrine given substance and the force of the law by the US Supreme Court in the Plessy vs Ferguson case of 1896.

The Question of his admission was sent to Texas Attorney General, Grover Sellers, who announced on March 16, 1946, that he decided to uphold "Texas' wise and long continued policy of segregation."

As such, Sweatt could apply for legal training at Prairie View, the Black college affiliated with Texas A&M University, and if no training were provided, then he could legally attend The University of Texas. In Sellars' view, a suited law curriculum could be set up at Prairie View in <u>48 hours</u>.[12]

Wiley College became fully accredited, so all who helped that to come about in their own way, helped in Hemans efforts because without that status, he would not have had the necessary credentials to apply to U.T. Law School. <u>Note</u> also, that the same was true of Langston University, in Oklahoma where Ada Lois Sipuel Fisher graduated before her application to Oklahoma University Law School. Credit must be given to any and all who helped those colleges to be accredited. Without that, the NAACP strategy would have been fatally flawed.

<u>The Factors in This Sequence</u>
WILEY COLLEGE; became accredited in 1933
A.P WATSON; this Author's father, was professor at Wiley College and chairman of the E. Texas branch of NAACP

PROFESSOR TOLSON - DEBATE TEAM

W.J. DURHAM; attorney with Thurgood Marshall for Brown v. Board of Education. Also handled a case for the Watson Family

---

[12] Nolan Anderson, Heman's fellow biology major from Palestine, TX. He later went on to study medicine at Meharry Medical School in Nashville, TN and returned to Marshall and became a much-revered physician and social activist.

HOUSTON BAHAI' COMMUNITY; Enrolled Heman in 1944, before his application to UT.

LOUIS GREGORY

ADA SIPUEL and the UNIVERSITY OF OKLAHOMA POST OFFICE; angered Heman when they bypassed him and promoted a "White" employee instead.

HARRY TRUMAN integrated the US MILITARY and appointed FRED VINSON as chief justice of the US Supreme court in 1947, he wrote the opinion in the Sweatt vs. Painter case.

The State of Texas reversed its bias against Blacks by establishing a school for Blacks. Texas Southern University opened its doors in 1947. Later the state began soliciting out-of-state, Black students to attend University of Texas.

DWIGHT EISENHOWER appointed EARL WARREN as chief justice of SCOTUS, he wrote the opinion in the Brown vs. Topeka case.

UNIVERSITY OF TEXAS – Brande's mother, Lena Watson, was refused entry to UT but the University paid for her to go to the University of Denver. Brande himself went there for a short while, as well as his daughter and grandchildren.

Each of these was necessary to bring the U.S Supreme Court to the decision in the Brown vs. Topeka case, nullifying segregation in public schools and facilities.

By action of the University of Texas System Board of Regents on August 13, 1987, the historic "Little Campus on the University of Texas at Austin was renamed the "Heman Sweatt Campus" in honor of Heman Marion Sweatt, a civil rights pioneer. A graduate of Wiley College in Marshall Texas, Mr. Sweatt also attended the University of Michigan and applied for the admission to the University Of Texas School Of Law in 1946. Denied admission because of his race, Mr. Sweatt brought legal action against the university, in the landmark case of Sweatt vs. Painter. The United States Supreme Court ruled that separate law school facilitate could not provide a legal education equal in quality to that available at the University of Texas School of law one of the national ranking law schools. That ruling established an important precedent for desegregation of graduate and equal doctrine the court affirmed Mr. Sweatt's rights to equal education opportunity and in 1950, he entered the University of Texas School of Law subsequently.[13]

In its September 17, 2001 issue, Time magazine recognized The University of Texas School of Law to be the national leader among schools working to broaden their traditional applicant pool. The article pointed to various efforts at UT Austin as exceptional, including the enlistment of high-profile minority alumni to write minority applicants encouraging them to apply, and the request by state senator that airlines donate tickets to bring out-of-state African Americans to visit the campus.

The Texas Exes alumni association gave nearly $ 400,000 in financial aid to 31 Hispanics 28 African Americans and one Native American in the academic year 2000-01.

UT School of Law in 2001 had more than 650 African American alumni and 1300 Mexican-American Mexican alumni, a group that includes such notable figures as Dallas Mayor Ron Kirk and former Secretary of Transportation Frederico Pena, also the one-time mayor of Denver. But this kind of representation was hard won. Equal opportunity and diversity came slowly and at a price.

Fifty years ago, lawsuits fought by Thurgood Marshall and the NAACP opened the doors of UT law school to African Americans. It was a long fight that began when the plaintiff in

---

[13] Mr. Sweatt earned the M.A degree in social work from Atlanta University and served as an official of the NAACP and the Urban League in Atlanta.

those suits, Heman Marion Sweatt, walked into the law school on Feb.26, 1946 and attempted to register for classes.

At the time, Sweatt was a 33-year-old Houston mail carrier who was married to his high school sweetheart. As local secretary of the National Alliance of Postal Employees, he worked with attorney Frances Scott Key Whitaker to prepare documentation in a case concerning discrimination against Blacks in the post office, the work sharpened his interest in the law as a means of challenging discrimination, and in 1945 he decided to go to law school. The Sweatt timing was perfect. The NAACP was formulating plans for a major lawsuit against The University of Texas.

The Sequence

Heman Marion Sweatt of Houston, Texas attended Wiley and majored in biology, aspiring to become a medical doctor. He graduated in 1934, thus he graduated from an accredited college.

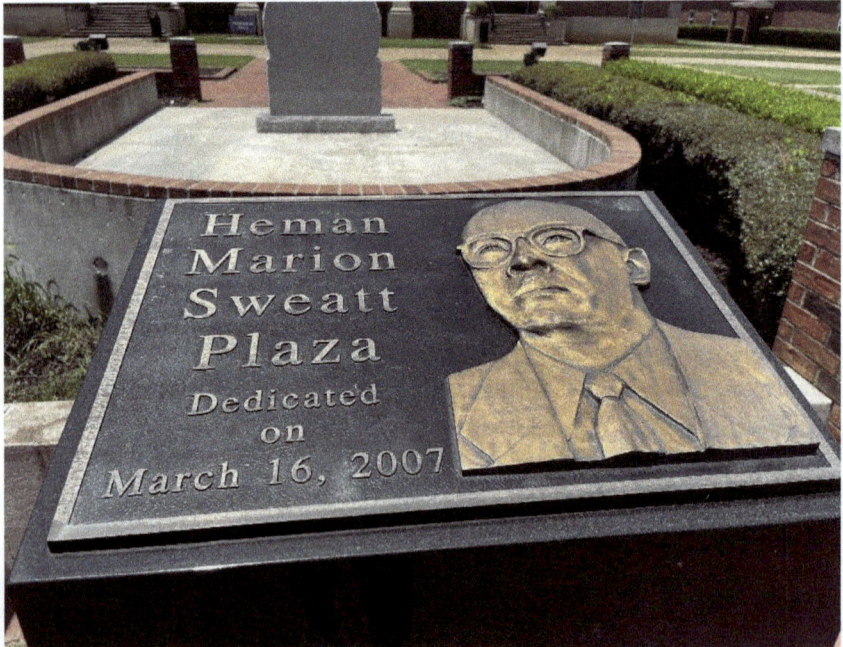

Image source: Used with permission from Wiley College

40

The NAACP in its efforts to prompt the U.S. Supreme Court to overturn the separate but equal doctrine that prevailed in schools and universities in the country, had won cases in Missouri and Oklahoma. Yet equal treatment was not accorded to the Black or minority students. Louis Gregory, the pole star of the race amity movement, which was sponsored by the Bahá'í community, had given up his own practice of law and accepted his invitation to conduct a series of events in Houston in the spring of 1944. His events sent a wave of uplift and unification through the Houston area.

Heman Sweatt declared himself to be a Bahá'í in the spring of 1944. It was in the summer of 1945 that he decided to forego his ambition to be a doctor and be the lynchpin that the NAACP needed to apply to the University of Texas Law School. Brande's father, A.P. Watson as professor at Wiley and president of the east Texas chapter of the NAACP coordinated the inter-relationships between these two main factors.

Due to a vacancy on the U.S. Supreme Court, President Harry Truman appointed Fred Vinson as chief Justice. It was Vinson who wrote the opinion that overturned the separate but equal conception and mandated that the state of Texas admit Heman Sweatt to the U.T. law school. President Dwight Eisenhower appointed Earl Warren as Chief Justice who in turn wrote the opinion in the Brown v. Board of Education which broke down racial segregation in all public schools and public places.

Thus, Wiley College, the NAACP, and the U.S. President, were all vital to the breakdown of racial segregation.

## Harry Truman and Fred Vinson

President Harry S. Truman, in his own way, had a beneficial effect on this thrust in more than one way. Truman is to be credited for his decision to integrate the U.S armed forces in 1947, and his appointment of Vinson as Chief Justice of the Supreme Court Knowing his disposition against segregation.

The Healing Racism workshop, put on by Rita Starr, were small gatherings where sharing of experiences fostered closeness, that in turn created empathy which led to united action.

Here is an excerpt from the book "To Move the World" by Gayle Morrison:

"In the mid-1940s, Houston, Texas. A Modest home. 8-10 adults, both black and white. A special guest, Mr. Louis Gregory, a distinguished brown-complexioned man in his early 70's comes and speaks movingly to the assemblage about spiritual matters. Heman is there. Louis Gregory's story presents a rich tapestry that invites deep and thoughtful study. He was a lawyer, one of the "talented tenth", yet he gave up a promising career to devote his energies full-time to spreading the teachings of the Baha'i Faith throughout the United States. He knew and associated with virtually all of the black leaders of his day-educators, clergymen, heads of civil rights organizations and many leading whites as well. 'Noble-minded, golden hearted', he was widely known as a lecturer and writer on racial unity. He stood in the forefront of every struggle the American Baha'i made to establish race amity."

# Chapter 12: Sweatt v Painter et al Decision

In the "Sweat v Painter et al" case the court documents show, "Petitioner was denied admission to the state-supported University of Texas Law School, solely because he is a Negro and state law forbids the admission of Negroes to that Law School. He was offered, but he refused, enrollment in a separate law school newly established by the State for Negroes. The University of Texas Law School has <u>16 full-time and three part time professors, 850 students</u>, a library of <u>65,000 volumes</u>, a law review, <u>moot court facilities</u>, scholarship funds, an <u>Order of the Coif affiliation</u>, many distinguished alumni, and much tradition and prestige.

The separate law school for Negros is <u>five full time professors, 23 students, a library of 16,500 volumes</u>, a practice court a legal aid association and one alumnus admitted to the Texas Bar; but it excludes from its student body members of racial groups which number eighty five percent of the population of the State and which include most of the lawyers, witnesses, jurors, judges, and other officials with whom petitioner would deal as a member of the Texas Bar. *Held*: The legal education offered petitioner is not substantially equal to that which he would receive if admitted to the University of Texas Law School; and the *Equal Protection Clause of the Fourteenth Amendment* <u>requires</u> that he be admitted to the University of Texas Law School."

It was a <u>mandate</u>, the much-sought compulsion that the previous cases lacked. The last sentence provides the leverage that the NAACP lawyers had ardently sought for over a decade to scuttle the "separate but equal" doctrine which an earlier supreme court had created.

# Chapter 13: The Stump

"The Stump" was located at the center of the campus. Cemented over, some students took to standing on the stump when making their points and opinions known, again, the professors encouraging this free thought and exploration of the students. "The Stump" and the interactions around it had great influence in how the students were treated in the classrooms.

The professors and students alike would gather around "the stump" at Wiley College to discuss their thoughts and ideas, as peers. The students were lauded for their ideas and thoughts by the professors.

# Chapter 14: A New Classroom Paradigm

There is now enough historical data to identify peoples by human or divine qualities such as, hospitable, courageous, scholarly, artistic, loyal, thrifty, cheerful, brave, clean, and reverent. (Remember some of these from the Boy Scout Law?) The other ideas are to reflect more accurately what is generally known about others and about ourselves, the identity of our forebears, what they stood for, what they did, and how they regarded and treated others.

<u>This is work</u>! But, like the analogy of the black and white piano keys, humanity must learn to recognize the synergy between us; the interaction and cooperation that creates a human master-piece. The plain notes of the white keys and the interesting inflections of the sharp and flat black keys make that possible. Indeed, the musician would be hard pressed to even find the desired keys without the black/white orientation. Each distinct people group demands a moral station of respect. Together, we produce a tapestry, and become color rich chord in a grand symphony. Now, history takes on a whole new dimension and significance.

While it is generally acknowledged that altered values of succeeding generations is a reality of all societies, the disconnects that occurred in the 1960's and 70's were more profound than usual, due, in great measure, to the stresses of the Civil Rights movement and the Vietnam War. While it was desirable, that certain traditions and relationships under-go changes.

Freedom, though highly prized, became license when it transcended the limit imposed by the rights of others. Responsibility became its casualty. Respect for elders was increasingly sacrificed at the altar of self-seeking waywardness. A dysfunctional counterculture began to emerge which used its abundant resources to indulge more deeply into mindless vices. Conveniences drugged the moral consciousness. How could this idea be defended? The children are not the problem; rather they are the prizes to be reclaimed. Teachers and schools have near impossible task of helping students with such vacuous backgrounds to achieve academic standards, with little or no corroboration from the home environment or religious exposure.

The vital need now is for a study guide, for an inclusive course, which would feature the Afro-Latino-Sino and Indigenous experiences on this continent, not as idioms or anomalies, but as integral weaving of fabric of American history. The lifestyles and interrelationships of these identifiable groups should be emphasized in such a way that all children will see themselves as co-inheritors of a rich legacy.

This is not just a "nice thing", but a moral imperative which would enable us to bring to bear not coercive power, but collaborative power which is suited to the task before us. Unvarnished history, that is a concordance, can give perspective that our young people need in order to reach transcendence from faulty tracings in the footpaths of their forebears. The new generation can prevail to enlightened engendering of a new society. Even an anthology of achievements, in all areas of endeavor, cannot fulfill this objective.

Maxine Hong Kingston, in conversation with Bill Moyers, once described the human condition in an interesting way. I believe her point was that history changes; not the facts themselves, but new information gives fresh context and import to our understanding of the human drama.

The Texas Alumni Association gave nearly $400,000 in financial aid to 31 Hispanics 28 African Americans and one Native American in the academic year 2000-01. UT School of Law currently has more than 650 African Americans alumni and 1300 Mexican-American, Mexican Alumni, a group that includes such notable figures as Dallas Mayor Ron Kirk and former Secretary of Transportation Frederico Pena, also the one-time mayor of Denver, but this kind of representation was hard-won. Equal opportunity and diversity came slowly and at a price.

46

# Chapter 15: One Stands Alone

While humankind has various dependencies for living and for health, because truly no man is an island, the Creator has no such reliance or need for support. This was once eloquently described by Kay Wilson. Brande says it in this way: that God has goals and purpose for all of His creation. He spoke purpose for His manifestations, His revelation, for all of mankind and for His faithful followers. This is shown in various cultures, as Tablets were written to different people groups, as meaning and understanding was enlarged each time. Baha'u'llah told us more about Who God is.

He taught that God is myriads upon myriads of kingdoms higher than we are. And nothing can keep Him from achieving His purposes, because His power is over all. With the understanding that new powers were gained every time our atom reached a higher kingdom, it made sense that God is the highest possible Kingdom, and therefore the most powerful and knowledgeable.

"Nothing whatsoever keepeth Him from being occupied with any other thing… Verily His ways differ every day." "He is established upon the throne of 'He doeth whatsoever He willeth' and abideth upon the seat of 'He ordaineth whatsoever He pleaseth.'"

Since all evidence points to the fact that God is orderly and intentional; we see that He assigns specific purpose to His creation. It becomes even more important for us to understand God's purposes, in order to cast off confusion, and also to better understand our Creator.

Abdu'l-Baha, who is the true exemplar of Bahá'í Faith explained, "Existence is of two kinds, one is that of God and beyond our comprehension. He had no beginning. He is All-Independent", He added.

Grasping how anyone could have had no beginning yet exist was beyond capacity. But not that He has all power. What does He mean to do with it, beyond creating the universe?

"God's purpose in manifesting Himself is to draw all mankind to the truth and to virtues." (G.299). So, God revealed Himself in order to lead us home to Him.

God created the universe for humanity, for we are the only creatures in it capable of recognizing God. His love for us must be astounding for Him to do all that for us!

God has "no desire but the regeneration of the whole world, and the establishment of the unity of its peoples, and the salvation of all them that dwell therein." (G.243)

What a noble purpose; and wholeheartedly desirable! He wants everyone on earth to draw near to Him and to love Him! That would indeed make this a new earth.

All souls are on a journey back to the Creator. God purposes to "to attract the souls, through the sublimity of His Words, unto the summit of transcendent glory and to endow them with the capacity of perceiving that which will purge and purify the peoples of the world from the strife and dissension which religious differences provoke." (TB.72)

"So powerful is the light of unity that it can illuminate the whole earth… This goal excelleth every other goal. Our supreme purpose and highest wish hath always been to disclose the glory and sublimity of this station." (ESQ.14-15)

These passages help us to understand God's purposes for us. Baha'u'llah explained, in a prayer: "When Thou didst purpose to make Thyself known unto men, Thou didst successively reveal the Manifestations of Thy Cause, and ordained each to be sign of Thy Revelation among Thy people, and the Day-Spring of Thine invisible Self amidst Thy creatures, until the time when… all Thy previous Revelations culminated in Him Whom Thou hast appointed as the Lord of all who are in the heaven of revelation and the kingdom of creation, Him Whom Thou hast established as the Sovereign Lord of all." (AHW#3, P&M.128)

Then it is through His Messengers that He communicates with people. They each in turn guided and educated us. God has always covenanted with His people to guide and prosper us if we obey Him. He periodically—about every thousand years—has sent us a new Guide to teach and unify us. Among Them are Noah, Hud, and Salih (mentioned in the Qur'an), Abraham, Moses and His Minor Prophets, Christ, Krishna, Buddha, Zoroaster, Muhammad, and, for our own troubled day, with the mighty task of unifying the entire planet, the Bàb and Baha'u'llah.

Baha'u'llah also likened the Prophets to physicians who "Foster the well-being of the world and its peoples, that, through the spirit of oneness, they may heal the sickness of a divided humanity." They alone "can claim to have understood the patient and to have correctly diagnosed its ailments." (G.80) God's purpose": To guide the erring and give peace to the afflicted." (G.81)

Oh, wouldn't it have been wonderful if their people had accepted them all in turn when they first came? We would have avoided millennia of sufferings. Yet, God leaves freedom of choice with us. He waits for us to love Him enough to accept His wisdom and to want to work with Him to establish His Kingdom and peace on earth...

Baha'u'llah said of the Prophets, "These Mirrors will everlastingly succeed each other, and will continue to reflect the light of the Ancient of Days. They that reflect Their glory will, in like manner, continue to exist for evermore, for the Grace of God can never cease from flowing. This is a truth." (G.74) What a promise!

Baha'u'llah prayed, "When Thou didst purpose to unveil Thy sovereignty and to glorify Thy word, and to reveal Thy bounteousness and mercy. Thou didst raise up one of Thy servants… choose Him above all Thy creatures… single Him out for Thy purposes… clothe Him with the robe of Thy guidance… immerse Him beneath the seas of Thy majesty and grandeur, and didst sanctify Him from all that beseemth not the greatness of Thy glory and the power of Thy might, and didst bid Him to cry out before all that are in heaven and on earth, and summon the multitudes to the Manifestation of Thy Self and the Revealer of Thy signs." (P&M.96-7)

As enlightened ones before him, Baha'u'llah did all this for meaningful reasons. Baha'u'llah said in a prayer that God purposed for His Manifestation" to: (numbers added)
1. Demonstrate the powers of God's sovereign might
2. Glorify God's Word,
3. Guide the steps of the people
4. Fulfill God's testimony unto all created things

"Each of these Manifestations hath been the bearer of a specific Message, entrusted with a divinely- revealed Book and been commissioned to unravel the mysteries of a mighty Tablet. The measure of the Revelation… had been definitely fore-ordained." "Every Prophet… hath been… charged to act in a manner that would best meet the requirements of the age in which He appeared." (G.74, 79-80)

Thanks to Baha'u'llah Who gave us two Interpreters to help us to understand. He said the Prophets are One, sharing the same Holy Spirit Who, like a ray of sunlight, brings enlightenment from God, the 'Sun of Reality'. He went on to tell us that the Prophets have equal rank. They restate more clearly God's eternal truths and meet the needs of Their time. They do this by bringing specific new messages to the people, as they develop and are able to grasp and use them. These a later Messenger may change as human needs change. The human race has been growing up the way a child does. But when the Bàb appeared, mankind "attained the stage of maturity." (G.77) And became able to receive this vast new Revelation.

This explanation can easily clear up dissension and quarrels between the various religionists.

Baha'u'llah summarized: "God's purpose in sending His Prophets unto men is twofold. The first is to liberate... men from the darkness of ignorance, and guide them to the light of true understanding. The second is to ensure the peace and tranquility of mankind, and provide all the means by which they can be established." (G.79-80)

He added, "The Divine Messengers have been sent down and Their Books were revealed, for the purpose of promoting the knowledge of God, and of furthering unity and fellowship amongst men." (ESW.12)

"At one time We spoke in the language of the lawgiver; at another in that of the truth-seeker and the mystic." (ESW.15)

Once humankind matured enough to comprehend Him, Baha'u'llah was able to speak in those and numerous other modes.

We are able to understand that every form perishes eventually, even the earth itself. However, the next world will be eternal. Humankind is offered eternal life near God. There is where we learn how to fit into such a glorious existence. Yes, we are responsible for caring for our planet. We have neglected and infirmed it for so long that we are in danger of destroying it. Yet, compared to the eternal higher kingdoms, Baha'u'llah said, "The whole world, in the estimation of the people of Baha, is worth as much as the black in the eye of a dead ant..." (ESW.124)

That brings us back to our priorities, our purposes. "Thou art God's shadow on earth. Strive, therefore, to act... as befitteth so eminent, so August a station," Bah'u'llah affirmed. (G237)

Next, Baha'u'llah explained that "Our sole purpose in raising the Call and in proclaiming His sublime Word is that the ear of the entire creation may, through the living waters of divine utterance, be purged from lying tales and become attuned to the holy… exalted Word which hath issued forth from… the Maker of the Heavens and the Creator of Names. Happy are they that judge with fairness." (TB.21)

I believe we are to clear our minds of the old interpretations that men of earlier centuries developed. In their attempt to understand the world around them, they had to work from the level of development at which they resided. In earlier times, Scriptures were understood too literally. We have to broaden our insight to receive the depth that the enlightened ones came to share and prepare us for His heavenly family and be at ease there.

He fleshed out that map into a picture to use as a guide. It begins: "Behold, a light hath shone forth out of the morn of eternity, and lo, its waves have penetrated the inmost reality of all men… Man, the noblest and most perfect of all created things, excelleth them all in the intensity of this revelation of man… He hath focused the radiance of all of His names and attributes, and made it a mirror of His own Self. Alone of all created things man hath been singled out for so great a favor, so enduring a bounty." (G.65)

"The purpose of God in creating man is but for him to know Him," the Bàb said. (SB.62)

Baha'u'llah also said this, adding, "And to attain His Presence To this most excellent aim, this supreme objective, all the… divinely revealed and weighty Scriptures unequivocally bear witness. Whoso hath recognized the Day Spring of Divine guidance (Himself) and entered His holy court hath drawn nigh unto God and attained His Presence, a Presence which is the real Paradise, and of which the loftiest mansions of heaven are but a symbol…

"Whoso hath failed to recognize Him will have condemned himself to the misery of remoteness… which is naught but utter nothingness and the essence of the nethermost fire." (G.70-71)

Then, when Bah'u'llah says He reflects God to us, He really does it. The fortunate people who gained entrance into His physical Presence, attested to the power and glory they found reflected in His face.

The Bàb also said God wanted humans' power of perception to be enhanced, "that the people may discover the purpose for which they have been called into being. In this Day whatsoever serveth to reduce blindness and to increase vision is worthy of consideration." (SB. 62)

Baha'u'llah added that keenness of understanding is due to keenness of vision. (TB.35)

It seems this 'vision' is spiritual perception, as physical blindness does not keep people from drawing near to God, or understanding His teachings. Many times, blind people are the most spiritual.

Then, both heaven and hell must be inside the human heart. We choose which to experience. We don't need to remain in the condition of nothingness. We can recognize God's latest Manifestation, Bah'u'llah, Who perfectly reflects God to humankind, and invites Him into our hearts. This is as near as we can come to God's Presence in this world, now that Baha'u'llah has ascended to the next world.

"He… chose to confer upon man the unique distinction and capacity to know Him and to love Him—a capacity that must needs be regarded as the generating impulse and the primary purpose underlying the whole of creation." (G. 65)

Here, it seems we are called to be humble and yet recognize our nobility. He wants us to realistically recognize who we are and who we are not. It is our connection with God that transforms us from being mere perishing shadows, to becoming God's beloved children. With His love in our hearts, we can become noble, exhibiting the virtues He placed within us. However, if we skirmish to rise above our station by arguing with God, or by opposing His Will, we will discover that we, in ourselves, are powerless. He said of this 'mere reflection',

"O SON OF SPIRIT! I created thee rich, why dost thou bring thyself down to poverty? Noble I made thee, wherewith dost thou abase thyself? Out of the essence of knowledge I gave thee being, why seekest thou enlightenment from anyone beside Me? Out of the clay of love I molded thee, how dost thou busy thyself with another? Turn they sight unto thyself, that thou mayest find Me standing within thee, mighty, powerful and self-subsisting." (AHW#13)

Is prayer the method Baha'u'llah gave us for making a meaningful connection with God? Christ told us, to "seek and ye shall find". (Mt7:7) It is a promise. So, it is imperative that we actively seek Him, and persist until He is found, no matter how long it takes, we cannot relinquish. Once we find Him, it is not to rest on our laurels. Earthly interests could blind us to His important purposes. We need to polish and develop our innate gems of patience and persistence, and open our hearts to receive His light purely, so that we can reflect Him on to others. He said, "if thou seekest another than Me, yea, if thou searchest the universe forevermore, thy quest will be in vain," "For none but Me can ever suffice thee." (AHW#15,#17)

Baha'u'llah said how to proceed: "The Word is the master key... inasmuch as through its potency the doors of the hearts of men, which in reality are the doors of heaven, are unlocked." (TB.173)

"The heart is the throne, in which the Revelation of God the All Merciful is centered... 'Earth and heaven cannot contain Me;

what can alone contain Me is the heart of him that believeth in Me, and is faithful to My Cause'..." (G.186)

Is this new Revelation the World? Or is it Baha'u'llah Himself? Jesus was called 'the Word'. (Jn.1:1, AHW#59, G.184)

This may mean that heaven is how I feel when I open my heart and welcome God in. Being All powerful, God, is too powerful for me to approach Him without being consumed. But His rays of love and life reflect onto the hearts of all who let Him in. His love is another key to the door to heaven.

Confirming this I found," They say: 'Where is Paradise, and where is Hell?' Say: The one is reunion with Me, the other is thine own self..." (ESW.132)"

# Chapter 16: All Others Do Not Stand Alone

As proof we can look to the development of every human embryo. We each begin as single cell in a vast universe- the womb. Each embryo has within it the wisdom (DNA) about what it is to become, as it divides again and again. The new cells that result from the process take on differing qualities- forming specific parts of the body. In the beginning the parts are independent, marked by self-importance. As the body continues to progress and develop the various body parts become specific in function, connected by the nervous system. The parts begin to interact to provide the body capacity beyond the comprehension of any of its parts.

The cell develops into a tissue, then an organ/s, then a physical being, then a human. "Then what?" This is what every human must ponder and answer. The cell develops with no concept of its relationship with the other cells. The tissue develops with no concept of its relationship to other tissues. The organ develops with no concept of its relationship to the other organs. The physical being develops with no concept of its relationship to other physical beings. The human develops with a concept of its relationship to the humans and God!

The cell creates a bond with like cells and becomes tissue. The tissue creates a bond with its like cells and becomes an organ. The organs start a bond with the other tissues and organs and create a physical being. The soul bonds to the physical being and develops a human. Then the human does what? The human strives to bond with other humans and God.

In fact, its first test as a system is to work together well enough to ensure the survival of the body. Doctors tell us that the development of the body includes bridging a point at which, absent this unity of the body's various parts as a system, the fetus will die before birth. This analogy is a "decision" of the body to unite and become functional and mutually supportive. It is similar to the decisions now being foisted upon mankind at this point in its development. Virtually all identifiable groups in American society have a role to play including various hate groups. Although, they are mostly "high stool drop-outs". They must carry out their function in the out-house, not in the living room, just as a healthy body must rid itself of waste.

So, the developing embryo matures from a group of specialized cells to a thriving fetus whose specialized parts must work together to survive. In that same way, humanity may have thought of itself as a bunch of individual nations that can vie for power and control over the others. We are moving into an age where the realization of our inter-dependence becomes evident.

# Chapter 17: Declaration of Dependence

Money as a controlling power over relationships between peoples. It has been used to keep people at odds with one another. If we become unified, that unity is greater than the power of that money.

This country has a moral mission which it cannot abort. It is the same as that which impassioned the framers of the U.S. constitution. Teachers in particular must show their suitability for fostering this uplifting approach to the learning process. Schools and teachers have shown that they can raise a child's vision from the banal to the sublime. The vital need now is for the integral weaving of the fabric of American history. The lifestyles, worldviews, and interrelationships, of these identifiable groups should be emphasized in such a way that all children will see themselves as co-inheritors of such a rich legacy.

This is not just a "nice thing" but a moral imperative which would enable us to bring to bear not <u>coercive</u> power but, a <u>collaborative</u> power which is suited to the task before us. Unvarnished history that is, a concordance, can give the needed perspective that our young people need in order to reach transcendence from a faulty tracing in the footpaths of their forebears, to enlighten engendering of a new society. Even anthology of achievements in all areas of endeavor cannot fulfill this objective.

# Chapter 18: From Educational to Learning Institutions

Wiley College is one that has plans to broaden its ambiance of learning as well as education, so that accumulation of relevant knowledge incentivizes students (future alumni) to take the helm in mobilizing our communities toward unity on some of its wedge issues. This would sparkle up the whole campus and highlight the interdependence of all the academic disciplines.

The suggestion is this: Regarding a divisive issue, debate teams would gather facts, rationalize thoughts, qualify authorities and conclusions with the aim of arriving at the best solutions to overcome preconceived notions and selfish interest, thus the competition would be to determine the team which concludes most competently not necessarily which can overcome the others' argument. After the presentation, the teams would conflate their summaries to refine their recommendations to pertinent govern- mental authorities in order to focus the community and thus eliminate the waste of endless partisan, sparring, fluff and scandal. In this way, everyone wins, including the community. As in football training, the "scrimmage" is not for one side to win, but to develop strength, skills, scrutinizing ability, and a game plan. With Wiley's resurgence on the college debate scene, she can set tem- plate for other colleges by this confluence of debate and dialogue and advances the American experiment with democracy in this global village in a fashion that would do honor to the memory of her iconoclastic Professor, M.B Tolson Sr. Wiley College has decided to adopt the Quality Enhancement Plan (QEP) topic "Communicate Through Debate", this is to encourage students' critical thinking skills through the use of debates. This will be an instructional strategy that will vastly improve and strengthen their communication skills. Wiley College is citing numerous studies that prove that students learn the principles of argumentation and prepare appropriately by researching and practicing in eager anticipation of debating, their cognitive skills and performance as well as their oral delivery. This aids in students developing confidence and greater literacy. These skills lead the students to become active team members, insightful leaders, and knowledge-able citizens.

The motif that runs through the American experience is the dynamics of the interrelationship between the skin-privileged and the dispossessed. What is vitally needed is a "whole cloth" study that does not marginalize the roles of non-White people or treat them as a footnote in history. Rather we must see the vital and indispensable threads in the entire fabric inclusive of some of the unconscionable exclusions and distortions that characterize so much of the record, and which have fostered and engendered an embedded sense of preeminence in the thoughts and actions of "White" citizens. Yet, more is required than purely reactive protest and politics. A profound shift in our collective consciousness must occur, a shift that makes possible a new America. The American nation, Bahá'ís believe, will evolve, through tests and trials to become a land of spiritual distinction and leadership, a champion of justice and unity among all peoples and nations, and a powerful servant of the cause of everlasting peace. This is the peace promised by God in the sacred texts of the world's religions.

Dean Earl Harrison of the University of Pennsylvania Law School testified that in the "modern system of instruction," the professor does not lecture so much as direct a discussion among the students. The larger and the more diverse the student body, the more powerful the teaching tool. Even outside the classroom, rubbing elbows with other students, taking part in small discussion groups, discussion with advanced students, all are very important considerations.

**Analytical Intelligence:** namely, analytic thinking is what most intelligence tests measure and undergraduate education emphasizes; examples include <u>knowledge acquisition and ability to execute a task</u>.

**Creative Intelligence:** Creative insight; being <u>able to see something old in a new way</u>; being able to combine different types of experiences in insightful ways; "ability to deal with novel tasks and situations…"

Wiley College monuments in honor of: Dr. Oliver Cromwell Cox, Prof. Melvin Beaunorus Tolson, Sr. and Prof. Andrew Pol Watson, Sr.

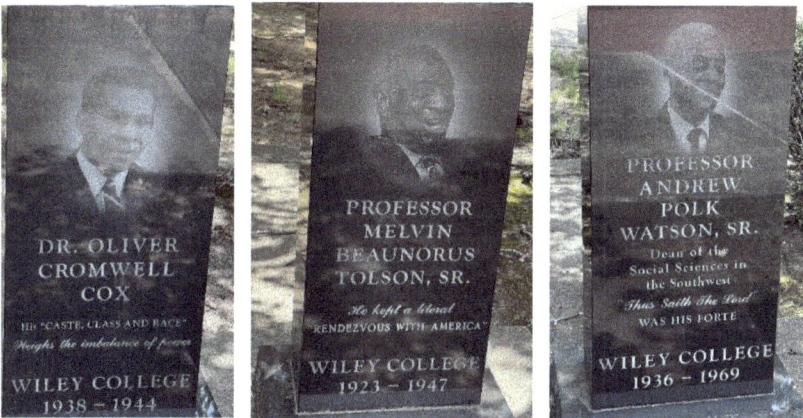

Image source: Used with permission from Wiley College

**Adaptive Intelligence:** Learning how to adapt to one's environment and when not to adapt; knowing when to change to meet needs; (<u>knowing how to "play the game" is street smarts</u>). In the middle of Wiley College campus is a cement covered tree stump. From time-to-time small gatherings of students, along with certain professors, Watson, Tolson, Cox, Morton, and Edmonson, would gather around the stump to discuss community matters and concerns. It was apparent to Brande, even as an on looking child, that they all spoke as peers and not as authoritarians. These episodes were a precursor to the new classroom paradigm whereby diversity and debate enhance the learning process and enable the spirits of all students to be mutually supportive.

# Chapter 19: Ezekiel Saw the Wheel

The hub of a wheel is that which encapsulates core values and principles the sense of worth, direction of goals, and connectivity to the source of power. However, it has a short radius, so for each turn it can move the wagon only a short distance. On the circumference, those political, economic, social, religious, or cultural groups in the community at large, coalesce to advance their ideas of improvement. The rim has a large radius, but it has little power to turn and move the cargo, for as it spins it puts one of the subgroups or another in the rut. Only when the center and the circumference are connected by spokes can there be the necessary interrelationship between principles and circumference – and you and others of us traverse the spokes. Thus, we are the spokesmen, in the church, we used to sing: "Ezekiel looked up and saw a wheel way in the middle of the air. The little wheels run by faith and the big wheels run by the grace of God". This is our wheel of fortune, right here on earth, which can transport us toward the heavenly realm.

Abdu'l-Baha, the True Exemplar of the Bahá'í Faith says: "This diversity, this difference is like the created dissimilarity and variety of the limbs and organs of the human body, for each one contributeth to the beauty, the efficiency and perfection of the whole. When these different limbs and organs come under the influence of man's sovereign soul, and the soul's power pervadeth the limbs and members, veins, and arteries of the body, then the difference reinforceth harmony, diversity strengtheneth love, and multiplicity is the greatest factor for coordination."

A Farmer has many gardens, one with corn, another with beans, a potato patch, tomatoes, carrots, and a field for grazing cattle. Each has particular vitamin which could sustain life for a while but alone cannot overcome diseases. But when put into a pot of water, heat applied and stirred – behold a wholesome stew. How many seeds in an apple? Five. Now how many apples are in a seed? If the seed is smashed, swallowed, thrown out, or thrown into a river there are none. Just like the Wisdom of Manifestations of the Supreme is refuted, ingested, rebuffed, or admixed with other learning, it is lost in the shuffle. If planted in fertile ground, watered, nurtured begins to transform the earth closest to it into roots which seek nourishment, and which then sprout and grow into fertile trees that will bear multitudes of fruit.

It is propitious now to fully explore the historical roots of how our populace is intermixed and inextricably interrelated. All of us have at least 92% of the human genome pool according to histological scientists. Look at the range and variety of colors and features of the people around you. If a 'back to Africa' movement had been carried out literally, there would not be a human being left on this continent.  Every identifiable group of humankind, whether of ethnic, religious, color, and/or creed variable, has a documented record of noble achievement – if we were but to look at the full picture. And every one of them has had members who brought that group to shame. Thus, whenever one segment of our society is extolled by speakers and writers, the protagonists for separation among us will counter with fulminations against them because the weak and fearful among us want to be identified with the groups that have temporal power. All students must learn how "race" was developed as a legal identity for discrimination by governmental agencies of all levels, that lightness and darkness of skin color and hair came to be used as a basis for people to determine how to treat each other, and that many people self-identify in order to avoid stigma and privations. They must also learn, as part of this fabric, how White-identified people worked and sacrificed for their oppressed fellowmen. Though "race" is generally recognized as the line of demarcation, the real action is between those of whatever color who want community and the benighted ones who seek sanctification under a veil of self-righteousness.

Perhaps the most illustrious of all historians, Arnold Toynbee, has studied the rise and fall of 21 of the world's greatest civilizations. He noted some stark similarities in their rise and demise. They began with a visionary, followed by the organizers, then the builders and later the aristocrats who consume wealth but have no memory of how that wealth was created. The vision was lost, and decline began, until total collapse occurred. This nation has followed that same path and is recognized as the single most powerful militarily and economically that currently exists. Yet that power not only cannot alleviate the most vital and challenging issue facing the country, but it may also contribute to separation. A sweeping denial begins to assert itself. Even though "Whites" may acknowledge the sufferings of minorities they generally are unaware of this baleful legacy.

Throughout America's history racism has been a cruel reality built into the very fabric of the nation. Whether by conscious choice or by callously ignoring its existence, the White ruling classes perpetuate the effects of racism against the Black and Brown residents. However, from slavery times, until now, there have been some brave individuals who seek to follow their higher selves and see the humanity in their Black brothers. Similarly, there were courageous Black people who stepped out on faith to defy the restraints put on them. In some cases, they were called to trust White individuals to not betray them.

So many people that call themselves liberty loving Americans try to assert a sense of superiority.

Thousands of 'outstanding citizens' actually lynched other 'outstanding citizens' because their skin tone was different than their own.

Countless scientific inventions are held up in pride. But the originators of so many of those products were Black inventors; and those facts have been hidden.

Professor Watson's wife faced obstacles as well. Despite her academic success, the University of Texas did not want to accept her into their student body. The university's work-around was to pay her tuition to matriculate outside of the state. She got her Master's degree from the University of Denver. The University of Texas later honored her, after denying her entry to their institution. Their son, this author, Brande Watson, went to the University of Texas Law School.

Brande was not spared the ugly truth of racism. When he was seventeen years old, he was driving a 1948 Buick. It was his day off from work. He and his brother took turns working for the downtown pharmacy. He was driving in Marshall, TX and looking for a parking space. It was a Saturday morning and he planned to wash and polish the car. He remembers the date, it was August 17, 1950. He drove around the courthouse near the store, where he was going to buy car wax. He stopped to allow a driver to leave the parking space. When the driver saw that Brande wanted the space, the middle-aged Caucasian driver decided to stir up a little trouble for fun. He stopped & asked Brande, "Do you want this parking space?" Brande replied, "Yes." The driver grinned, "Well, you ain't going to get it." Another guy came out and colluded with the first guy to attack Brande. The other guy walked over to Brande & saw a hunting knife in Brande's car. He backed up and told the police Brande had a knife. The police came and asked Brande for the knife. Brande bent over to get it and the cop hit him on the back of his head with the butt of his gun. Several Whites passers-by stopped and gathered around. He told Brande to get out of the car. They took him to jail and then to the courthouse, on the same day. Like many young Black men before him and many after him, Brande was about to be railroaded and very well could have lost his life. His Dad was a college professor & headed the local NAACP. When his dad arrived, things took a positive turn and Brande was spared. They wanted to charge him with carrying a deadly weapon & assault.

Before this incident happened, it was assumed Brande would go to Wiley College, but after this experience, the football coach of Texas College asked his father to send Brande to Texas College. Because they knew that Brande had been singled out & those people would continue to pursue him until they either killed him or put him in prison, his parents sent him away to college. The football coach knew that Brande was not the kind of kid that would have run from the situation.

There was another, first-hand experience that Brande had as a young man. In his early 20's, after serving in the military as a Ft. Bragg paratrooper, Brande went to Detroit to look for a car. It was February 1956. On the way back to Texas, to finish his boards, he felt sleepy driving. He was going through Houston, Kentucky and it was around 2-3AM. He found a gas station & stopped to sleep. The station was closed. It was dark and there was no traffic. Fast asleep, he snapped awake when police rapped on the car window with his gun drawn. "Damn nigger" the cop repeated several times. He reached into the car & slapped Brande. That was a moment of decision. It was life or death. Brande had been removed from the car. The cop had his gun in his left hand and slapped Brande with his right. Brande's first thought was to kick him, but he had removed his boots to sleep. Had he followed his instincts, he would have been shot on the spot. The cop looked for drugs and kept calling him a 'damn burr headed nigger'. Had he resisted, or responded, he would have been shot & buried in Western Kentucky.

Gone to Sandusky

One form of resistance remained consistent throughout the scourge of slavery. Some kidnapped persons sought liberty by escape. Empathy and kindness are not relegated to one group of people. There were some Whites who recognized the cruelty of slavery and would assist escapees to make a successful run toward "free" states or to Canada. The institution of slavery had its own vocabulary. There were words to describe various parts of the trade for people. There were also words and phrases for the administration of rebellion. During the time of the mid to late 1800's, when White southerners crossed the Mason-Dixon line, looking for escaped slaves, they had a phrase for the unclaimed. If the formerly enslaved person couldn't be found, they would say, "They're gone to Sandusky".

Sandusky, Ohio was a place that had a few ravines, a rather flat, topography, and some dedicated abolitionists. Runaways could find passage to New York or to Canada with the help of Sanduskians. Some abolitionists would train the escapees in different skill sets, so that they could be known as a technician or someone with a specific educational background – therefore, they were not a slave. So, if someone was missing, and search parties

have searched high and low, but that Slave was nowhere to be found, they would say, "Give it up, they're gone to Sandusky."

White sympathizers in Sandusky wanted to help; and this was their way of helping. They would train runaway slaves in a freed man trade. The escapee could then attempt to disclaim any accusation of being a slave. Some of these Black tradesmen could then move on to other locations to establish themselves, if they knew someone in the new town that could help them avert the slave trackers and patrols. Some stayed in Sandusky, Ohio.

Sandusky was a major station in the Underground Railroad and had the code name, "Hope". The Underground Railroad was a network of people who had both the dedication and the ability to help enslaved people escape, and to move through certain pathways to free states in the north. These abolitionists worked tirelessly to secure escapees along the route to a safer location. One such person was Rush Sloane, who was an attorney and mayor of Sandusky. He was instrumental in helping many escapees. He was tried and fined, under the 1850 Fugitive Slave Act. Unlike some others, he did not lose his life for that conviction. This town was a place where runaways could go and cross over Lake Erie into Canada.

Another wealthy, White sympathizer who wanted to assist as many enslaved people as he could, had a former slave, who was his assistant. The assistant would identify people who wanted to take the very perilous path that could possibly lead to their freedom. There were times when the assistant was mistaken for a slave and was captured. He was once taken to the trade block to be sold. His partner, the White abolitionist, bought him back at the auction.

# Chapter 20: Power Greater Than Money – New Race

The <u>new race</u> of men is composed of people of all colors and cultures of mankind involved in a <u>new race</u> toward civility along a track divinely ordained. The baton passed on to willing souls. What will public history and private diaries record of that passing? <u>What is the "whether report"</u>?

Christ taught His beleaguered followers, "Ye must be born again, not that ye come again from your mother's womb. That which is born of the flesh is flesh. That which is born of the spirit is spirit."

When schools arise to incorporate all elements of a good educations as <u>de rigueur</u>: reading the historical record, applying logic and reason, understanding values and objectives of the community, adding to the record, and discovering who they are, we will see a paradigmatic shift from self- serving ego to the world-serving brotherhood. A New Race of Men will appear, not colorless and bland, but colorful and vibrant, united in the spirit of our national motto: "E Pluribus Unum." The study of history must never be the same.

**The New Race of Men:**
1. People who go beyond the myth of race. Interracial marriage, folks who helped slaves escape.
2. It's not being color blind but rather "color full".
3. The marching in the street chanting "can't breathe" "hands up don't shoot" these marchers represent the new race of men.
4. Because of this new race of men, we will have from one – a fabulous diversity. We must work together to build this new democracy in America.

5. We celebrate the declaration of independence. Soon we will celebrate the declaration of <u>inter-dependence</u>.

Now several questions arise, and you can show your shape. Have you broadened your repertoire of interpersonal communication and cultural creativity? How will you use your position, powers, and capacities to bring about greater unity to deal with the ills that afflict mankind? Who are your allies? Will you realize your full potential as a unique creation? Will you adorn the pages of future histories?

More than a hundred years ago, Baha'u'llah, founder of the Bahá'í Faith, addressing heads of state, proclaimed that the age of maturity for the entire human race had come. The unity of humankind was now to be established as the foundation of the great peace that would mark the highest stage in humanity's spiritual and social evolution. Revolutionary and world-shaking changes were therefore inevitable.

Democracy, which means the people rule, was put forward as the ideal governing modem. The U.S. Constitution was patterned after that of the five Iroquois Nations of N.E. United States and S.E. Canada.

The Founding and formation of the U.S. is comparative to different gardens, each with a special vegetable, gathered and put in a pot, each with a particular nutritional value. They are gathered in one pot, heated, and stirred.

The cells that evolved into mankind over many millions of years had within themselves the "plan", so to speak, of what they would become. Every person, without exception, went through that same developmental process while in embryo for approximately nine months. As the cells form into vital functions, so groups of people organize in order to increase capacity. Just as the vital organs reach a point of "decision" as to whether or not to support one another, so humankind is at that point at the present hour. The bone of contention is whether to augur for success of the entire body or to be born dead in the next world.

# Chapter 21: Science and Religion Agree

Science and religion must agree. This is the major premise of the Bahá'í teachings.

Science is the study and comprehension of all physical matter that has corporal existence, mixtures, changes, interrelationships, and consequences. Mankind develops language to describe all the phenomena and the uses of "things" to suit his purpose.

Religion is the revelation and comprehension of the spiritual or non-physical influences and capacities of mankind. The Revealers of these understandings come from "heaven" above and acceptance of the laws and principles they bring is dependent on recognition of their sublime status. Thus, their teachings are based on that belief and thus they have faith.

All that we can see, hear, touch, taste, and smell in this corporal existence gives us a language by which to describe reality of our corporal world. Religion, revealed to us by the Prophets of God, in accordance with the capacity of mankind to understand at the time of each One's appearance, uses the language of the corporal world to teach us spiritual realities.

Humanity today is like an orchestra without a conductor of a common score. The various musicians may each be able to play his or her instrument well, but without unity of purpose (that the conductor and music score provide) it's impossible to listen to the resulting cacophony. It's only when the conductor takes the stand and leads the members of the orchestra in a musical score, they can all see and play that the noise stops, only then can the concertgoers enjoy the beauty of the music. The composer is akin to the Divine Creator who evinces His plan for mankind through religion which is progressively revealed through a succession of Prophets, who, not only do not compete, but sacrifice their mortal lives to unfold more of the Plan. Compare this to how you were taught simple words to express primal experiences and feelings; then were taught

ABC's by the 1<sup>st</sup> grade teacher; the second grade teach uses those building blocks to teach you new words, and then the third-grade teacher uses all the previous learning to teach sentences, then paragraphs.

In chronology of religions, a faction of people fixates on a particular teacher (conductor) and denies the legitimacy or equality of previous or successive Ones, even while receiving benefits that each of them left to the world.

Whether conveying feelings or ideas, the process is very much the same. This may explain why Jesus alluded to fishing to fishermen, carpentry to carpenters, and farming to farmers, all to convey the same spiritual concept. The reason why there is a physical world, and we have concrete experience is so that there is a language whereby the Prophets may communicate with us about spiritual realities.

# Chapter 22: Embryo - Birth After Death Eye to I

From the writings of Abdu'l-Baha, "The power and comprehension of the human spirit are of two kinds, that is, they perceive and act in different modes. One way is through the organs, for instance, the eyes and ears. The other manifestation is the powers and actions of the spirit that operates <u>without</u> instruments and organs. For instance, in the sleep state, it sees without eyes; without ears it hears; without feet it runs. Think of how often it happens that in a dream, one can "see" a happening and its significance becomes clear years later. In the same way a question that cannot be resolved in wakefulness is solved in the world of dreams. In this manner, a person can "see" their deeper spiritual self without.

The new race is comprised of the people who are bound together in spirit by love of justice, trust, truthfulness, sincerity, service to mankind, and are inextricably bound to mankind's dire need for unity.

During this century a power greater than ravenous war has evolved, and that new dynamic is money, corporate wealth. It has been estimated that the 26 wealthiest men in the world own and control more financial resources than 3.4 billion of the poorest people on earth. Plutocrats determine whether there should be war between nations and/or violent outbreaks within communities which redound to their economic advantage. According to presidential hopefuls, three wealthy families control more wealth than the lower half of the U.S. population.

It has been revealed in the Bahá'í writings that power much greater than any that has been known before is being uncovered and spread throughout the entire world. In my humble opinion, this means a "significant" percentage of the world's population situated in all corners of the globe will be so committed to the principles of <u>unity and justice</u> that they will eschew all criticism of anyone.

Rather they will acknowledge the energy and power which denigrates and destroys and show how that same force can be redirected in mutually beneficial ways.

# Chapter 23: One Religion

Almighty God created the endless universe, and then created mankind to learn about that vast world. And in so doing they would get to know Him better progressively and to relegate or reunite with Him.

The progressive revelations of that religion can be compared to a school with successive grades. For example, in grade one the prophet, or teacher, would teach people the ABC's; then in the second grade, that teacher would instruct the students how to rearrange the letters to make words; in the next grade they made sentences, paragraphs, then whole stories. That prophet even told the synagogue that he was Moses and Moses was he (Jesus).

The Bible recounts that after Moses led the Jews to the promised land, God spoke to him and said, "I will raise up one like unto yourself from among your people." Moses and Jesus were one.

Humanity must recognize that we're all on the same team. As in football, a squad forms teams which play against one another, not so much for one side to win, but to develop skills and talent for contests with other high schools. The same is true for colleges, not solely for sports, but for debate. So that society may more strongly unify and function at its best.

As fires, floods, tornados, and eruptions increase the threats to annihilate massive numbers of people, mankind will be forced to unify and become entirely interdependent, just as each of us did while in embryo. The world is at a point of decision-making.

# Chapter 24: Religion is One

God created the endless universe and put mankind in it to learn about Him, and to worship Him.

It is like a school with progressive grades. The teachers are known as prophets. In the first grade they are taught the a,b,c's ; in the second grade how to make words, the third how to make sentences, and so forth.

Just as the "schools" are the same religion at progressive levels, the "teachers" are the occurrence of the same spirit. For example, the Messiah came to assist the Hebrew people. When He urged them to love one another, they accused Him of being contrary to Moses, He told them "I am Moses and He is me."

Also, in the fifth book of the Bible, God is quoted as saying to Moses "I will raise up one like unto yourself from among your people."

These examples of 'oneness' implicate the concept of one God, one religion, one prophet and one people, who must learn that they are one and interrelate on that basis.

# Chapter 25: Declaration of Dependence

People of today are astonished to learn of aircraft, obviously from other planets that come to earth and can fly at rates twice the speed of sound. Art worked with a significance yet not known or agreed upon, has been carved into mountain sides.

There is speculation that religious practices, such as painted faces and bodies, the wearing of feathers and of exotic dances around the fire were influenced by space travelers from other worlds.

Of the three hundred Indian tribes situated throughout the North American continent, the six populated by the Iroquois were recognized as the most culturally advanced. They were all located near the Great Lakes region of the United States and Canada. The Framers of The Declaration of Independence were stymied at certain aspects of the task, and taking note of the unity of the Iroquois tribes, sought the help of the chiefs. When it was completed, the head chiefs of the Iroquois tribes were invited to the hearing before the U.S. Congress, and at least one chief attended.

# Chapter 26: Identity

Who am I? God is to be known and appreciated by humans. Therefore, He created the physical world so mankind may learn to subsist, and by analogy develop an understanding of spiritual realities. For instance, we learn that a magnet attracts metal to itself. This is true in the physical science. In the spiritual world, this is an expression of how loving hearts are drawn together.

The soul. It has within it all our true identity and reality. One of God's purposes is for us to educate it to be happy in higher kingdoms near Him by detaching it from the earthly things that hold us back.

Human life consists of body, mind, soul, and spirit, yet we do not know when the latter three begin or end.

Why am I? Our souls are "eternal, unchanging spirits are the essence of life, which is love, a breath from God, and so perfect, giving each body life. It receives the light from God's Holy Spirit." This is something which, we are divinely taught, is the purpose of our existence and experiences. The more we get together the more we get it together.

Many thousands of years ago there were animals on the European continent with large horns growing on their heads. People learned that if they cut off those horns and blew through them, they made a pleasant sound. People in Asia living by pool and lakesides noted reeds and noted that by covering some of the holes they could create beautiful sounds as they blew through them. In Africa during those early times, when large beasts were killed, their skins were spread out and, when beaten, provided a rhythm to which medicine men would dance. They would wear exotic paintings on their faces and bodies and would dance to discourage sickness and evil. Eventually, composers arose to use the sounds and refined instruments to create classical music which can, and does, stir deep emotions, in players and listeners around the world. Here we see unity, in diversity, in a classic example of inter-dependence worldwide, in scope and in significance.

As to the question, "Why are we?", the answer is clear. It is to promote unity, inter-dependence, and mutual trust among the people of the world and advancement of justice among all mankind.

Ponder for a moment the needs of the faith in its God given directions to minister to the dire needs of a suffering humanity: to visit and solace the hungry and dispossessed; to send pioneers and settlers to raise up the administrative order; to vastly increase the financial resources; to teach and to love with divine inspiration; to be resolute in our convictions; to thrill the hearts with memorable and moving gatherings.

This is the day of the "many sheep" who must be gathered in "one-fold" by the Lordly Shepherd, as Christ said He must do. We are about our Father's business when we are among the brethren.

# Chapter 27: Mankind is One

Can there be pain without suffering? Consider a mother giving birth, an athlete winning a grueling race, a martyr… Is there suffering without pain? A mother who sees her child die, a soldier who fails in carrying out a mission; an athlete losing after knowing he did not do his best.

Some people understand that bringing about true equality is not just a matter of acting "nicey nicey." Instead, it is a crucial dynamic that is necessary to establish true interdependence and benefit everyone.

Think of a deck of cards. <u>The backs of the cards</u> are all the same, symbolizing that all are exactly equal in importance. The faces of the cards are all different, for instance the spades, though different in rank, represents the capacity of mankind to develop wealth from the earth. Clubs, develop the capacity to make weapons and therefore control the spades. Diamonds represent the capacity of mankind to develop trade and commerce and thereby multiply the value of the wealth.

What remains is the hearts which represents the spiritual nature of mankind and the capacity to show love and compassion and carry out what must be a divine calling. Consider a farmer who has many fields of crops. He gathers crops from each field and puts them into one pot and turns up the heat. Each of the crops has a particular nutritional value, each one of which can preserve certain aspects of a person's health, because of oppressive treatment of different lands; people sought refuge in a new continent.

Race is often misconstrued with nationality (place of birth), linguistic heritage, and religion. With race being a biological term, it technically applies or refers to none of these things. There is only one scientifically accepted definition of "race". Race refers to a biological sub-division of a given species, members of which inherit physical characteristics which tend to distinguish that sub-division from other populations of the same species. However, scientists realize no matter how precise you make the definition, there are no clear sub-divisions in the single species of man, *Homo sapiens.* There are more people in the categories between the sub-divisions than belong to the sub-divisions themselves. It is common for an individual to have characteristics which place them in several categories at once. Therefore, the more traits that we use as a form of classification, the more races are found. Scientists have made statements on the number of races ranging from two to two hundred.

Most scientists agree that all humans are descended from the same ancestors. These ancestors most likely lived between 600,000 to 1,000,000 years ago. Furthermore, scientists agree that a "pure" race of man has never existed and therefore will never exist. The reason for this is the extensive migration and inter-marriage that has taken place since the beginning of the species.

Anthropologists classify the various races by selecting one or more of the obvious physical traits exhibited by different races. The most common traits used are shape of the eyelid, hair texture and color, shape of the nose, head shape, skin and eye color, and stature. However, rather few people fit these categorizations of the "ideal" of any race since there is so much overlapping. For instance, the tallest person of a short race may be taller than the shortest person from a tall race. Additionally, the darkest-skinned person of a light-skinned race may be darker than the lightest person of a dark-skinned race.

Every piece of scientific evidence supports that all races have identical capacities for intellectual success. Although the similarity of intellectual capacity is only fairly measured if all peoples have the same and equal opportunities for health, security, and education in the broadest sense of the word. Every race has individuals that are highly intelligent and gifted, as well as those who are less intelligent. No evidence exists that shows that natural selection has been functioning in any way to produce a distinct difference of mental capacity or talents in any specific race.

All civilization at the height of their ascendancy thought of themselves as everlasting. They were wrong… And they were right. The regimes crumbled, but the culture survived and passed off their world views to later generations for the advancement of the global community. The great strength and vital contributions of Blacks and other minorities is not military or political might but moral change or a keener sense of justice, each sector appreciating and celebrating the unique value of all others. 'Whites cannot do it alone. Blacks cannot do it alone. They must do it together." (Rev. James Forbes, on News Hour). The cultural abyss is too wide for rapprochement without an underlying sense of common destiny. When schools arise to incorporate all elements of learning as de riguer: reading the historical record, applying logic and reason, understanding the values and objectives of the community, adding to the record, and discovering who they are, we will see a paradigmatic shift from self- serving ego to world-serving brotherhood.

From mankind's early beginnings there have been people who envisioned and sacrificed for a unified society. In America today rising numbers of peoples are drawn together by chords of affinity.

A passage from Abdu'l-Baha states:
"In the beginning of his human life man was embryonic in the world of the matrix. There he received capacity and endowment for the reality of human existence. The forces and powers necessary for this world were bestowed upon him in that limited condition. In this world he needed eyes; he received them potentially in the other. He needed ears; he obtained them there in readiness and preparation for his new existence. The powers requisite in this world were conferred upon him in the world of the matrix so that when he entered this realm of real existence, he not only possessed all necessary functions and powers but found provision for his material sustenance awaiting him.

Therefore, in this world he must prepare himself for the life beyond. That which he needs in the world of the Kingdom must be obtained here. Just as he prepared himself in the world of the matrix by acquiring forces necessary in this sphere of existence, so, likewise, the indispensable forces of the divine existence must be potentially attained in this world.

What is he in need of in the Kingdom which transcends the life and limitation of this mortal sphere? That world beyond is a world of sanctity and radiance; therefore, it is necessary that in this world he should acquire these divine attributes. In that world there is need of spirituality, faith, assurance, the knowledge, and love of God. These he must attain in this world so that after his ascension from the earthly to the heavenly Kingdom he shall find all that is needful in that eternal life ready for him.

The divine world is manifestly a world of lights; therefore, man has need of illumination here. That is a world of love; the love of God is essential. It is a world of perfections; virtues, or perfections must be acquired. That world is vivified by the breaths of the Holy Spirit; in this world we must seek them. That is the Kingdom of everlasting life; it must be attained during this vanishing existence.

By what means can man acquire these things? How shall he obtain these merciful gifts and powers? First, through the knowledge of God. Second, through the love of God. Third, through Faith. Fourth, through philanthropic deeds. Fifth, through self-sacrifice. Sixth, through severance from this world. Seventh, through sanctity and holiness. Unless he acquires these forces and attains to these requirements, he will be deprived of the life that is eternal. But if he possesses the knowledge of God, becomes ignited through the fire of the love of God, witnesses the great and mighty signs of the Kingdom, becomes the cause of love among mankind and lives in the state of sanctity and holiness, he shall surely attain second birth, be baptized by the Holy Spirit and enjoy everlasting existence. "

In the late 1960's Brande was visiting a dear friend in the Dallas area, and was asked if he would like to visit J. Howard

Griffin? He was somewhat startled because Griffin was the author of the book "Black Like Me". The book was so revealing of the Black experience that the author was targeted by racist bigots and his whereabouts were a secret. Brande readily accepted his friends' invitation, and they drove directly to the residence. Mr. Griffin greeted Brande as if he was a long-lost friend, He even demonstrated the intricacies of his residence.

Seeing Eye to I

Brande's first experience with Louis Gregory was in December 1953. It was his junior year of college at the University of Pittsburg. As Brande awoke in the pre-dawn hours, a figure appeared in the doorway, a tall slender man in a black double-breasted suit with white pin stripes, the man was behind Brande and yet he could see the man without turning. Not a muscle in his body would move, and even now Brande is not sure if he was asleep or awake. The man moved towards Brande without walking and made no sound and yet he conveyed that he was adopting Brande. He then moved back to the door, and when he was no longer visible Brande "awoke". Six years later, he learned about the Bahá'í Faith and became a member on September 30, 1960. In 1972 the Bahá'í community established the Louis Gregory Bahá'í institute in South Carolina, and Brande was appointed as the Dean of the institution in 1973.

One day while showing a film strip, there was a picture of the National Spiritual Assembly of the United States and Canada. In the middle of the picture was the exact image of the person Brande had seen in his epiphany experience nineteen years before. At that moment, he began to realize the significance of what had been conveyed to him 19 years before.

"Mah Brotha"

In the middle of the 1960s two Bahá'í buddies were travelling in east Texas, with Brande and visiting friends in that area. In the late afternoon they arrived in Longview and decided to have dinner at a restaurant. The public accommodations law had gone into effect a year or so earlier.

Both of Brande's friends were White, and one of them, Dar Bradshaw, with his grey eyes, balding forehead, slightly hooked nose, and fat tummy resembled a classic southern sheriff.

The young men decided on a restaurant, went in sat at a table and waited, and waited for a waitress. After maybe five minutes, one came over with two glasses of water and put them in front of the Whites, and then without a word turned and walked away. Dar, in red-faced anger rose and shouted loudly at her, "WHARS HIS WATAH!" The waitress was stunned, and perhaps all the other patrons were as well. "You don't disrespect this man! This man is MAH BROTHA!"

No one could move. To hear that from a man who looked and sounded like a southern sheriff was startling. He went on "Git the manager out here. I want to talk to him." The waitress said timidly, "He's not here." Dar replied, "Well get him on the phone, I want to talk with him!"

No one moved. Finally, Brande said, "Let's go!" He knew from his former days as a waiter, not to eat anything that was served by a waiter who disliked their customers.

As they drove away, it was obvious Dar had been affected by the experience. He didn't speak for the next hundred miles. Witnessing someone whom he felt so close to treated in that manner, gave him a keener insight as to who he was.

History Professor
In the 1950s Brande had a history teacher who had a small trailer home filled with memorabilia and artifacts of Afro American achievements. He attached it to his pick-up truck and travelled to communities throughout the south, wherever he could get himself invited, despite frequent threats from hate mongers. This was a White teacher. Brande's dad, who was a professor of the social sciences at Wiley College, and chairman of the East Texas Branch of the NAACP, welcomed him openly. The picture of these two marvelous men shaking hands made the local newspaper.

Andrew Carnegie Library

The most eye-catching building on Wiley College campus was the Andrew Carnegie Library. Not until his adult years did Brande know why it was so named. One day on a visit there he overheard the head librarian, Mrs. Gertrude Mason, explaining to a small group that the money magnate Andrew Carnegie contributed the entire sum of money for the construction as he did for several minority communities around the country.

A Walk with a Friend

One day in the late 1980s, Brande was visiting a friend, a White woman in her late 40s, a stage actress in the same group of which he was a member. It was a warm, sunny, Saturday afternoon and they decided to walk to a favored restaurant since it was only half a mile away. As the two of them walked along the dirt path beside the four-lane roadway, a car came along. As the car passed them, there was a light beep on the horn and a young White fellow leaned his head out the right-side window, smiling and gave them a thumbs up. As they passed, Brande and his friend could see at least four or five people, all White, in the car.

# Brande Watson

Bransford Watson: Oklahoman, 32, is civilian employe at Tinker Air Force Base in Oklahoma City, managing world-wide distribution of Air Force material. He pilots a small plane, mostly in the service of the Baha'i religious faith.

# About the Author

As an Adjunct Professor at Antioch University in Ohio, Bransford Holloway Watson "Brande", facilitated 'Healing the Races' dialogues and extended to communities around the country, achieving great success. He also promoted *Americans All,* a history series that illustrated the oneness of the human family. He coached the **Wiley College** debate team in Marshall, Texas (the movie, 'The Debaters' with Denzel Washington, was about the earlier years of the famous Wiley College debate team, in which his father Professor A.P. Watson, Sr. was involved). Mr. Watson was a Professor at Central State University and also taught French at Dayton Ohio High School. He served on the Regional Board of the National Conference of Christians and Jews. Mr. Watson was an Industrial Consultant for the Texas Commission on Alcoholism and Community Relations Assistant at the U.S. Department of Justice, during school integration in Texas. He also served as Dean of the Louis Gregory Baha'i Institute in South Carolina and was a member of the Baha'i National Teaching Committee. He was a District Patrol Officer in Houston, Texas, and completed a lecture tour in Siberian Russia. Brande Watson was a member of the World Congresses and took several pilgrimages to Haifa, Israel. He was once Ebony Magazine's Most Eligible Bachelor. Brande was a Double Sprint Champion in the NAIA competition, Debate Team and Track Team Captain at Texas College. His MBA is from University of Texas & his Bachelor's degrees are from Texas College, University of Pittsburgh and University of Oklahoma. His wife – Evelyn Watkins & his daughter – Brenda Oliver, Brande has four grandchildren. He was inspired and encouraged by his parents, Professor and Mrs. A.P. Watson, Sr. Brande Watson is a private pilot, theater actor, motorcyclist, lecturer, and writer who enjoys classical music. He is well-travelled.

www.ingramcontent.com/pod-product-compliance
Lightning Source LLC
Chambersburg PA
CBHW060808110426
42739CB00032BA/3140

* 9 7 8 1 9 5 4 0 0 8 0 5 2 *